You are
to be

immisation

MW01108995

THEN GOD SAID TO ME:
"I HAVE HIM"

A True Story of God's Supernatural
Visitation, Mercy and Grace

JUDY LAWRENCE McGILL

WESTBOW
PRESS®
A DIVISION OF THOMAS NELSON
& ZONDERVAN

Scripture taken from The Message. Copyright © 1993, 1994, 1995, 1996, 2000, 2001, 2002. Used by permission of NavPress Publishing Group.

THE HOLY BIBLE, NEW INTERNATIONAL VERSION®, NIV® Copyright © 1973, 1978, 1984, 2011 by Biblica, Inc.® Used by permission. All rights reserved worldwide.

This book is a work of non-fiction. Unless otherwise noted, the author and the publisher make no explicit guarantees as to the accuracy of the information contained in this book and in some cases, names of people and places have been altered to protect their privacy.

WestBow Press books may be ordered through booksellers or by contacting:

WestBow Press
A Division of Thomas Nelson & Zondervan
1663 Liberty Drive
Bloomington, IN 47403
www.westbowpress.com
1 (866) 928-1240

Because of the dynamic nature of the Internet, any web addresses or links contained in this book may have changed since publication and may no longer be valid. The views expressed in this work are solely those of the author and do not necessarily reflect the views of the publisher, and the publisher hereby disclaims any responsibility for them.

Any people depicted in stock imagery provided by Thinkstock are models, and such images are being used for illustrative purposes only. Certain stock imagery © Thinkstock.

ISBN: 978-1-5127-5542-8 (sc)
ISBN: 978-1-5127-5544-2 (hc)
ISBN: 978-1-5127-5543-5 (e)

Library of Congress Control Number: 2016914458

Print information available on the last page.

WestBow Press rev. date: 10/06/2016

CHAPTER 1

Thursday, July 10, 2014 was a terrible day. My husband Butch had been in the intensive care unit at Barnes Hospital in St. Louis, Missouri, for four days following a horrible accident, and the outlook wasn't good. I couldn't believe this was happening. It all seemed so surreal. However, I knew from experience that sometimes God allows us to suffer difficult times to help us to grow, to learn, or to be tested. Other times He allows us to endure these experiences to draw others closer to Him. And sometimes it's all of this and more. This is a love story—a love story involving husband and wife, parent and child, friend and friend, and most important, my heavenly Father and me.

"Here's another way to put it: You're here to be light, bringing out the God-colors in the world. God is not a secret to be kept. We're going public with this, as public as a city on a hill. If I make you light-bearers, you don't think I'm going to hide you under a bucket, do you? I'm putting you on a light stand. Now that I've put you there on a hilltop, on a light stand—shine!" (Matthew 5:14–16 The Message).

Powerful words. As Christians we are called to shine. The catch is that there is no guarantee that the light stand we are put on will be easy, beautiful, or painless. Sometimes we are called to suffer through difficult times in order to shine. People tell me that I'm strong. People I've known for decades—family members, coworkers, and acquaintances—have said this to me. Even strangers have told

1

me this. Many people have come up to me in public places and said, "Hi, Judy. You don't know me, but I've been following your story on Facebook. I've been praying for you. You are so strong." I guess they've seen strength in me that is hard to understand. Many people have told me that they would not be able to endure what has happened to my family and me.

My life story has been fairly public through newspaper articles, social media posts, and word of mouth. I have been a teacher in public schools for many years, so I know a lot of people, and a lot of people know who I am. My husband was the principal of the middle school in a neighboring district for most of his career in education and was a volunteer fireman in our community all of his adult life. People know us. Our story is public. It's a long, complicated tale that includes many trials, tragedies, and grief. So many times I've cried out to God. Sometimes my prayers have been answered the way I've hoped. Sometimes they weren't and the unthinkable happened. But this is the light stand on which God has placed me, and though it hasn't been easy, my desire has always been to shine for Him.

When Butch and I married, it was the second marriage for both of us. We had both suffered unwanted, painful divorces. I applied for a teaching position in the district where he worked. The circumstances that led me to do this were definitely arranged by God. I was finishing nursing school, even though I was already a teacher. After my divorce, I felt that I needed a change, and the nursing profession was an obsession of mine. But a friend had told me of an opening in this district, and after working at a hospital for more than a year, it became clear to me that a teacher's schedule would be much better for a single-again mom.

Butch and I already knew each other. We had participated in a Christian singing group in our younger years, and I had done my student teaching in his building. At the time, he was a teacher. We would pass in the hall and say hi, but that was about it. I had no idea when I applied and got an interview for a position that Butch was the principal. Because we knew each other, the interview was a little different than if we had been strangers. We shared information on a more personal level. We both had broken hearts and had no idea what God had in store for us in the near future. We both were single-again adults, raising two kids. We both loved God deeply and passionately.

After I started teaching in Butch's building, our casual conversations became more personal as we discussed our kids. Our friendship grew as we discovered how much we had in common. We spent a lot of time talking about our struggles and our triumphs, and our ties strengthened. Though Butch was my boss, our budding relationship had the support of teachers and the upper administration in the district. It's amazing how God can make things happen! He is a redeemer and wants what's best for His children. He loves us.

We were married a year and a half later, with our four kids as our attendants and the majority of district employees on hand. We were so blessed, but blending a family isn't easy. Butch's home had included a son and a daughter. Mine had included two daughters. Our two oldest kids—his son Joe and my daughter Tiffany—are two weeks apart in age. My younger daughter Jennifer and his daughter Kristi are about year apart in age. We threw everyone together under one roof. Poor Joe. He had to feel overwhelmed when three more females moved into his domain. All of the kids had to deal with their world being turned upside down, but we became a family. Siblings fought just like in a traditional family, but they loved each other as well. We had a fun, music-filled home with four extremely talented, intelligent, beautiful kids, and we were blissfully happy most of the time.

We didn't know that God's plan for us didn't include all rosy times. His plan was to thrust six people—two adults and four kids—into a life that would include tragedy, heartache, and pain as well as joy and happiness. But I believe He sometimes calls certain people to endure such times to show how amazing He is, thus putting us on a light stand. I feel honored to be used in this way, but it hasn't been easy.

3

We don't understand why God allows bad things to happen to us. Some would say I've had more than my share of tragedy. But in all of my life's difficult and even tragic circumstances, I've never once questioned God's goodness. My hope is that my story will show how our all-powerful, all-loving God never deserts us, especially when the storms of life threaten to blow us away. I hope to convince everyone reading this that He's still good, even when the depth of loss we experience takes our breath away. It's during those times that He shows Himself in ways that are miraculous and supernatural. He reveals Himself in ways that are hugely powerful, yet intimate. He makes Himself known in ways that cannot be explained away. He loves us so much! Before I continue my story it's important that I make one thing very clear: I'm not strong! The strength people have seen in me is not me, but Christ in me. I feel that I am anything but strong. Throughout all of this, my Lord carried me. And that's what is most important to know.

CHAPTER 2

I f we've lived long enough, it's natural to divide our lives into chapters, and my life's story has many. There is so much to tell about how God made Himself incredibly real by offering mercy and grace in the years before this part of my story began, but that tale will have to be told another time. I will start by introducing you to my wonderful mother. It's important that you get to know a little about her because she plays an important role in this story. She was one of those moms who lived for her kids. When my two brothers and I were growing up, she was focused entirely on us. My dad was a policeman who worked odd shifts, meaning we spent many afternoons and evenings with just Mom at home. She entertained us in creative ways. We didn't have much money, but I never knew that. Money wasn't an issue. We had lots of adventures and learned while having fun.

One of my favorite memories is of going to a harbor on the Mississippi River for dinner. We would roast hotdogs on a portable grill and play in the sand. Mom would take us for walks in the woods, and we would explore caves. All three of us kids were highly allergic to poison ivy, and though we could identify those three-leaved plants, we still often wound up with miserable rashes. We painted boxes and made them into houses that, in our eyes, were super cool. We painted rocks. Mom made clothes for me out of brand-new bedsheets. Hey, sheets are fabric, right? I had one-of-a-kind dresses on which she hand-embroidered flowers, making my dresses more beautiful than those worn by any of my friends. Her signature was an embroidered strawberry. It was the most coveted signature in my family, especially for my daughters. If something tore, a strawberry embroidered over it would fix it.

We had a beautiful Jonathan apple tree in our backyard. Throughout my childhood and my teenage years the fall was dominated by the production of all things made of apples. We would come home from school to find my mom, my grandmothers, and my aunts in the kitchen peeling and cooking apples. Oh the aroma! Apple pies, apple cobblers, apple crisps, stewed apples, applesauce—you name it, they were creating it in our kitchen. Then there were the fresh apples right off the tree. My mom made and froze apple treats for everyone. And she did all this with an enormous amount of love in her heart.

Of all the wonderful things my mother did for us, the most important and life-changing gift she gave was teaching us to love Jesus. She took us to Sunday school and church every week. She made it possible for us to be involved in youth ministries and Christian singing groups. I fell in love with and gave my heart to Jesus at a very young age. He was my comfort when the drama of junior high caused my heart to break. He was the one who carried me when I went through a divorce. He gave me hope when my younger daughter, at age two, was diagnosed with type I diabetes. He is the reason I have always had joy in my heart, no matter what was going on in my life. My mom is the reason Jesus was so real, because she introduced Him to me.

Mom was a smoker. She became addicted to cigarettes before it was known how bad they are for people's health. When she started smoking it was the cool thing to do. Everyone smoked. She had smoked cigarettes for decades before it was revealed that smoking causes lung cancer, emphysema, low birth weight in babies, and a plethora of other health problems. For her the addiction was emotional as well as physical, as is the case with many people, and for Mom, the emotional addiction was far stronger. By the time she finally was able to quit, she had suffered many bouts with pneumonia, requiring several hospitalizations over the years. Her lungs were severely damaged, and there was no way to heal them.

Smoking also can intensify the effects of osteoporosis, and my mom's spine would develop compression fractures from normal daily activities like sitting in a chair. She was often in a lot of pain. An X-ray exam would reveal how porous her vertebrae were—so thin you could barely see them on the film. Young people who start smoking today have the warnings that research has provided about how smoking damages the body. Most think that they will never suffer these horrible effects or that the threat is so far in the future that they can consider quitting later. But later seldom comes in time to prevent a lifetime of severe pain and difficulty breathing.

My mom endured several years of agony before her doctor found a course of treatment that helped to rebuild bone density and improve her breathing. As a result, she was able to stay in a beautiful assisted living facility where she made lots of friends and enjoyed playing games without having to be hooked up to oxygen. I am very thankful for the gift of those three years. Life had seemed to level out for my family and me. Everyone was content, healthy, and happy. My mom was in a beautiful facility and was very happy. Our kids were happy and settled into their marriages and careers. Our grandchildren were the most beautiful, talented, and intelligent children on the planet. All loved Jesus and served Him in their churches.

One evening in the middle of May I received a phone call. I was singing on the worship team at my church for a special prayer-and-praise service, and we had been rehearsing for a couple of hours before the service began. I didn't notice the voicemail message until about two hours after the initial call. The nurse's message was that my mom had tripped and fallen in her apartment. She was in the emergency room at a local hospital. I felt terrible that I hadn't noticed the voicemail earlier. Mom had been in the emergency room for at least two hours with no one to sit with her. I raced to be with her.

When I arrived, she was in an examination room, lying on a gurney, resting but in a lot of pain. It was apparent that she had broken at least a couple of toes on each foot, but the rest of her looked uninjured. A woman with broken toes is not as high on the triage list as patients with life-threatening injuries or illnesses. The emergency room was very busy that evening with people in apparently far worse shape than my mom, so she was positioned pretty far down the list to be seen.

Hospital emergency examination rooms aren't the best places to spend a lot of time. The beds aren't made for patients' long-term comfort, and the chairs for those waiting with them aren't either. We waited for hours without seeing a doctor—Mom on her gurney and me on my hard little chair. As we waited, we talked about nothing in particular, trying to pass the time. About three hours after I arrived, Mom's eyes went blank and she pursed her lips, making the most unusual sound, like she was blowing bubbles. I kept calling her name, but she wouldn't respond. I screamed for help. When the nurse ran into the room, my mom started to come around, but something wasn't quite right. She didn't know where she was or what day it was. Blood tests revealed she had thrown a blood clot into her lung. The staff immediately began to treat her with blood thinners, got her stabilized, and sent her to the intensive care unit. The condition of her lungs was not good to begin with, so this was an extremely serious situation.

This was the beginning of an ordeal that lasted about three months. Throughout this time, Mom was never able to return to her apartment, even for a day or two. She was admitted to three hospitals, had three stays in intensive care units, and was sent to three rehabilitation facilities. She was bounced from one hospital to a rehabilitation facility, back to a different hospital, and so on. She would get well enough to enter a rehabilitation facility where the goal was to get her well enough to return to her apartment at the assisted living facility, but her improvement never lasted for long. Every time she went to a rehabilitation facility, she would develop pneumonia, which would send her back to the emergency room, resulting in another hospital admission. Each time she was in the hospital she developed secondary infections, which would put her into contact isolation and back in the ICU. This cycle continued throughout the summer. If the situation sounds complicated, that's because it was. I felt so bad for her.

I was the only one of my mom's three children who lived near her. She and my dad had divorced years before, and he had passed away. One of my brothers lived a full day's drive south of us, and my other brother lived several hours north, so all of the responsibility for her care fell to me. I loved my mom and was honored to take on this responsibility. However, sometimes it was almost too much for one person. Fortunately, I had cousins who were willing to help during this difficult time. Without them I would never have been able to survive the storm looming on the horizon. I share all of this information about my wonderful mom and her health issues because it is extremely important in this chapter of my life's story. As difficult as it was to have my mom so sick and in so many health care institutions over several months, I had no idea how much tougher things would become, and very soon.

In the beginning of July 2014 after my mom had been in two hospitals and the first rehabilitation facility, the doctors felt that a fresh set of eyes would be beneficial, so they arranged to transport her to one of the best hospitals in the country, Barnes Hospital in St. Louis, Missouri. This is a teaching hospital where much research is being done in many areas. We were blessed to live just across the state line in Illinois, so even though people would come from all over the country to this hospital, it was only a thirty-minute drive from my house. This place is like a city. Its size is overwhelming, with a maze of overhead walkways connecting blocks of buildings housing doctors' offices, classrooms, St. Louis Children's Hospital, and other facilities too numerous to count. I felt good about Mom being sent there. Not only was the hospital highly ranked, but it was connected with the famed Washington University Medical School.

If there was help to be found for my mother, it would be found in Barnes Hospital.

Mom was placed in an attractive corner room on the ninth floor. Huge windows graced this room overlooking Forest Park, a beautiful spot directly across the highway from the hospital. Since this was July Fourth weekend, we talked about how we would enjoy watching the fireworks from her hospital room. She was also close to the hospital helicopter pad. People who were badly injured or gravely ill would be flown in regularly from accident sites or other hospitals. Whenever I called or came to see her, Mom would comment on how many helicopters she counted landing on the roof, delivering desperately ill or injured patients who were fighting for their lives. She liked to count things. During her numerous times in hospital emergency rooms through the years, she would pass the time by counting the number of ceiling tiles, floor tiles, or patterns on the wallpaper. If something was countable, she would count it. We often laughed about this. It was one of her odd personality traits. Artistic people are sometimes quirky. My mom was extremely artistic and extremely quirky. These traits were endearing, as was her unusual sense of humor. She could effortlessly produce roaring laughter in a room when she was in the right mood. Even during this marathon hospital stay she would sometimes have the staff in stitches. Everyone loved her.

Mom was resting comfortably during her first few days at Barnes, but the doctors weren't encouraging about her prognosis. End-stage COPD was not the diagnosis I wanted to hear, but this was the reality. I knew what this meant. Mom faced slow suffocation due to diminishing lung function. She was weak and tired of struggling to breathe and of being in pain. She had been in one hospital after another for close to two months. Mom began saying she wanted to go home. She was not talking about her apartment but about heaven. This upset me greatly, and I assured her that it wasn't time to start talking like this and that I needed her. I wasn't ready to let go of my mom. I had already suffered enormous, unthinkable loss. I hadn't fully recovered and felt I couldn't handle yet another huge loss. I know that we can never be ready for such a thing, but I wanted a little more time to heal before having to suffer through losing my precious mom.

On Sunday, July 6, Butch and I, my daughter Tiffany, and her husband Jeremy attended a St. Louis Cardinals baseball game. Busch Stadium is only a few miles down the highway from Barnes Hospital, so after the game the four of us visited my mom. She was an avid Cardinals fan and already knew they had won because she watched the game on the TV in her room. We had a good visit. She seemed comfortable and doctors were talking about sending her back to Illinois the next day to a different rehabilitation facility to try to help her get stronger. That was the story she had been told by the new intern on the floor. But the resident doctor on her case took me into the hallway and explained that she was indeed in end-stage COPD and that I should start considering hospice care.

I was not ready to hear this. I had seen Mom bounce back so many times before, and I had faith that this would be another one of those times. I believed that the next day she would be transported to the new facility, would begin her rehabilitation again, and this time would be successful. We hugged her good-bye and headed home after a very long day. On the ride home we discussed our plans for the next day, Monday. We needed to do some things around our house. My husband had just retired in early June from a long, wonderful career in education, so with my mom being in the hospital since May 18 and all of the retirement celebrations, we had neglected our summer household chores.

Butch was able to retire a little earlier than some because he had saved up so many sick days, which he could count toward years of service. This allowed him to retire a few months short of his sixtieth birthday. He was still pretty young! There were parties and celebrations, honors and awards to commemorate an exemplary career that made a difference in the lives of young people. For his retirement party in June I created centerpieces for the tables that included several versions of Butch's school pictures through the years sticking out from the arrangements on skewers. They became a great source of entertainment at the party. People took pictures of themselves with Flat Butch, inspired by the children's book *Flat Stanley*, written by Jeff Brown and Macky Pamintuan. There were pictures of Flat Butch eating cake, drinking punch, and sitting on people's heads.

One family in particular had the most fun with the Flat Butch shenanigans—Tyler, Janna, and their kids. Tyler and Janna are good friends of ours. Our daughter Kristi's fiancé, Jeff, decided it would be hilarious to pull a practical joke on Tyler and Janna by "forking" their yard with all of the Flat Butch skewers we could gather. It was awesome! We sneaked out later that night and covered their front yard with Flat Butch skewers. Tyler and Janna didn't see them until the next day. What a way to wake up! Tyler and Janna weren't going to let the prank die there, so they gathered up the skewers and for several weeks they transported Flat Butch all over the community, taking pictures with him at different landmarks and posting the photos on Facebook. This became quite a thing. It was fun to see where he would pop up next. The Flat Butch movement was born, but we had no idea the level it would reach in the next few weeks.

I have always been so proud of Butch. He is an amazing educator, administrator, fireman, father, and husband. And he is a powerful man of God, a prayer warrior. It's fun being the wife of a man who is well known and respected in the community. Sometimes God uses a man like this to get the attention of many people. We've always been eager to be used by God to reach people for His kingdom, but we didn't know how high the price could be or that the light stand God would put us on would be so difficult and painful.

Butch and I enjoyed working on projects together. He and I made a perfect team, complementing each other quite well. We knew we had little time to accomplish specific chores, because we were leaving for vacation that Friday. That left us only four days to make serious progress, but we were undaunted. Together, we were a force to be reckoned with. The plan was to get up, go to breakfast, shop for materials that we needed, return home, and get to work. It's amazing how quickly plans can change. The Bible says this: "Now listen, you who say, 'Today or tomorrow we will go to this or that city, spend a year there, carry on business and make money.' Why, you do not even know what will happen tomorrow. What is your life? You are a mist that appears for a little while and then vanishes. Instead, you ought to say, 'If it is the Lord's will, we will live and do this or that'" (James 4:13–16). How very real this Scripture passage was about to become for us—again.

CHAPTER 3

Monday, July 7

T he day started like any normal summer day. I am a teacher, so I was on summer break. Many people say that the three best parts of being a teacher are June, July, and August, but I love my job. And I love summer! We started the day with a leisurely meal at our favorite breakfast restaurant, Fiona's. The people there always greet us at the door and have our coffee ready practically before we sit down. I drink regular; Butch drinks decaf. He joked that it didn't feel like he had retired yet, because he would always be off in July. We had plans that day to order a new garage door and to buy stain for our deck in the back of our house. We enjoyed our breakfast, discussing what we would do that day and in the days to come. Interesting how we make plans, thinking we know how the day will turn out.

Leaving Fiona's with our stomachs full, we headed to Lowe's to order our garage door. We looked at many designs for doors, windows for the doors, and window embellishments. I was amazed at the choices that had to be made when ordering a garage door. We finally came to an agreement and placed the order. The next task on our agenda was to visit a hardware store that sold the stain we wanted for our deck. Our next-door neighbor's deck always looked amazingly perfect, so we decided to use the same stain he used. After purchasing the stain, we headed home. By this time I was ready for a little lunch, so I went to the kitchen and had a sandwich. Butch was doing something in the yard, so he told me to go ahead and eat. He would be right in. I finished eating and headed to the bedroom to change into my swimsuit so I could power-wash the deck, preparing it for the amazing neighbor-recommended stain that would create a beautiful finish.

I was half-finished power-washing the deck when a storm blew in with black clouds, wind, rain, lightning, and thunder. I turned off the power washer, pulled it under the eave of the house, and ran inside. The storm was clearly going to last awhile, so I stepped into the shower to wash off the deck debris stuck all over me. I finished showering, got dressed, and relaxed on the bed for a bit. Because Butch was a volunteer fireman in our community, things got pretty busy for him and the other firemen during the next couple of hours. Storms always create work for the firemen, with lots of emergency calls. Butch went out on two, but neither seemed serious.

After returning from the second call, he walked into the bedroom and said, "Hey, did you know there is a tree limb on our roof?" I had no idea. I hadn't heard anything hit the roof, so I was surprised. I went outside to look. The limb was still attached to the tree, so it didn't hit the roof but was brushing over it. The limb was fifteen to twenty feet above the ground. I snapped a picture and posted it on Facebook with a caption: "This could be a problem." Little did I know how prophetic that line would prove to be. Another storm was brewing on the horizon, and although it was a figurative one, this storm would be every bit as powerful, scary, and damaging as the natural storm that blew in earlier.

There is a common misconception that when we accept Christ as our savior, He will protect us from difficult circumstances, and so Christians are supposed to walk around happy and carefree all the time. Because of this misconception, many people become disillusioned or discouraged during difficult times. Some even give up on their faith when life gets tough or when prayers for healing or deliverance from problems aren't answered the way they want them to be. We may think our prayers go unheard when the outcome isn't what we expected. Sometimes healing doesn't come. Sometimes the dream job doesn't materialize. Sometimes a marriage doesn't make it. Jesus never promised that when we accept Him as our personal savior He will shield us from the trials and tragedies of this world. He never promised to give us everything we think we want. But He did promise to walk with us during difficult times. He promised us that we would have "life and have it more abundantly" (John 10:10).

Some interpret this to mean an easy life, wealth, or power. Some believe that if we have enough faith, God will give us whatever we ask. I'm not a Bible scholar, but I love Scripture. In the Bible God tells us, "Do not store up for yourselves treasures on earth, where moths and vermin destroy, and where thieves break in and steal. But store up for yourselves treasure in heaven, where moths and vermin do not destroy and where thieves do not break in and steal. For where your treasure is, there your heart will be also" (Matthew 6:19–21). I believe that the life Jesus promises must mean something far better than our worldly definition of abundance.

According to *Webster's Dictionary*, one definition of *abundance* is an ample supply. In a world where wealth is revered, it's understandable that the word *abundance* could be interpreted to mean wealth and many material possessions. But if this is what Jesus meant, why aren't all Christians wealthy and living in their dream houses with all the possessions their hearts desire? Is it because they don't have enough faith? Goodness no! Nice things are not bad, and it's not wrong to want them. But the God I've come to know intimately has so much more to offer than just the lowly riches of this earth! His abundance is much sweeter and far more satisfying. Nothing can compare.

We Christians are often accused of using God as a crutch. I'm okay with that. I'm weak. He is strong. Why wouldn't I lean on Him? Without that crutch, many people would have a difficult time surviving the storms that blow into their lives. I've experienced His abundance in some of the most difficult times in my life—times when I felt that I didn't have the strength to take another breath due to profound fear, loss, and sorrow. In those times the challenge was so great that I had no choice but to trust Him to carry me. The abundance I've experienced is His presence. God has made Himself real, tangible, and even audible at times. He's shown Himself to me in miraculous ways that cannot be explained away. The minutes, hours, days, and months became filled with my need for this abundance and this crutch. I don't think I would have survived emotionally unless God had carried me through what happened later that day and in the weeks that followed.

Butch's pager went off again, so he had to rush to another emergency. It was a quick call, nothing too serious. After everyone returned to the firehouse, Butch mentioned that he had a limb on the roof of the house. The fire chief asked if he should send a crew over to remove it, but Butch said, "No thanks. I've got it." The limb didn't seem like a big deal, and he felt he could take care of it. When Butch got home, Kevin, our neighbor with the amazingly beautiful deck, offered to help him cut off the limb. Butch went down the hill to our church and borrowed an extremely long ladder that we used to change light bulbs in the ceiling of the church auditorium. People don't usually own ladders this tall, so it was good to be able to borrow this one. Because of my post on Facebook, Butch received a few more offers of help with removing the limb from the tree. Again, Butch gratefully declined because it seemed an easy enough task with just him and Kevin. And he was right. They removed the limb without incident, cut it into smaller pieces, and carried most of them to the street to be collected by the village street department. Workers would come around periodically to check for things like that, and it was nice to have this service available.

Standing at the foot of the tree, Butch looked up and said he would like to remove another limb that might pose a problem in the future. Kevin agreed, so Butch again ascended the ladder. We don't know what happened after that. Kevin says he was holding the ladder and sawdust hit him in the eyes when Butch began cutting the limb. He dropped his head and didn't see what caused the event that followed. I was in the living room on the phone with the director of my mom's assisted living facility. The apartment had been held for her since her fall on May 18, and I assumed the director was calling to discuss what needed to happen regarding the place. The conversation didn't get very far. Kevin opened the front door and told me I needed to call 911 because Butch had fallen and was unconscious. I thought he was joking, because he seemed eerily calm. He assured me that he was serious and that I needed to call immediately.

The events of the next few minutes are somewhat of a blur. Seconds seemed like hours. My future life flashed before my eyes. I've heard of this phenomenon, but until that moment I hadn't experienced it. This thought resounded in my head: *I'm a widow.* I told the woman on the other end of the phone, who was a former student of Butch's, that my husband had been in an accident and that I needed to hang up. I was talking to her on my cell phone. I grabbed our landline phone and ran outside. What I saw will haunt me for the rest of my life. Only one other vision has had such a profound emotional effect on me, but that was something that happened in an earlier chapter of my life that I will have to write about another time.

When I ran out the front door, everything seemed to happen in slow motion. I saw Butch lying on the ground at the foot of the ladder. I remember hearing the chain saw still running. Tree limbs, leaves, and branches were scattered everywhere. Butch was unconscious. His eyes were half open, his complexion was gray, and he was gurgling. There was evidence that he may have hit his head. His body was mangled. I called 911, provided our address, and reported what had happened. When the dispatcher started asking questions, I yelled, "This is Butch McGill who has fallen. Get here now," and hung up on him. We don't know what caused the fall. We know that he was standing near the top of the ladder, trying to cut off the problem limb. As a fireman, Butch knew about ladder safety, so I doubt he was standing too far at the top. We suspect the chain saw got caught and kicked back, knocking Butch backward. Kevin didn't see him fall, but he saw him land. He fell fifteen feet and landed on his head and left shoulder. The chain saw landed on his chest, and the limb he was cutting landed on top of the saw. Kevin cleared those things off immediately and ran to get me.

We don't live in the fire protection district where my husband is a fireman, so the first responders who came to our house were not from the department where he served. However, we are very close communities, and the men from neighboring fire departments are part of a close-knit brotherhood. Everyone knows everyone. Everyone who responded to our house knew Butch extremely well. Some were family friends. Some were his former students. Some he knew because the fire and police departments that serve our neighborhood also serve the school district from which Butch had just retired.

While we were waiting for help to come, my neighbor across the street, who had experience as an EMT, ran to assess the situation. She knelt at Butch's head, held him in a C-spine position, and began talking to him, even though he was unconscious. I thought he was dead. He looked dead. And if he wasn't dead, it was apparent that he was severely, even gravely injured. Judging by the way he was twisted, his spine appeared to be broken. I looked at him, looked at Kevin, who now appeared to be in shock, and said, "Oh Kevin, this is bad. This is really, really bad, isn't it?" Kevin was unable to speak, but tears welled up in his eyes, and he simply nodded his head.

I knew I needed to call our kids—Joe, Tiffany, and Kristi. I was standing next to Butch when I made the first call, barely remembering how to find the number in my contacts. It's funny how we never memorize phone numbers anymore. I punched in Joe's name. He answered on the second or third ring. I told him that his dad had fallen from a tree and that the situation was dire. At this time I still thought Butch was dead. Apparently that's the message I communicated to Joe without saying as much. The tone of my voice said volumes. I asked him to make the other necessary phone calls because I didn't think I could. I made one more call, to Tiffany, because I knew she was the closest to our house, and I needed her.

I turned back toward where Butch was lying, and at that point something rose up in me. He had just retired a month before. We had three kids with spouses and four grandkids. We had plans. We were convinced God had plans for us. This was not what was supposed to happen. I couldn't continue alone. I needed Butch. I took a deep breath and knelt next to my mangled-looking husband, laid hands on him, and prayed, "In the name of Jesus, I ask, God, that you touch my husband's body right now and bring healing. Please, Lord, touch my husband!" I don't know who else was in my yard besides Kevin and our neighbor Leslie, who was holding Butch's head. Several neighbors were there when the emergency crew took him away, but I'm not sure when they arrived. Immediately after I cried out to God, those who were there witnessed Butch groan and move a little. He moved both arms and legs slightly but was obviously in agonizing pain. When we later learned the extent of his injuries, it was no wonder. I asked him if he knew who I was. Through labored breathing he whispered my name. He moved his arms. He moved his legs. He said my name. God is good and there was hope. It was a miracle.

When the fire department and the ambulance arrived, the slow motion stopped and everything became a whirlwind. When Tiffany turned onto our street and saw all of the rescue vehicles, she parked far enough away so that our grandson Logan, who was almost eleven at the time, wouldn't see what she feared to be a reality—his pawpaw lying on the ground dead. Leaving Logan in the car, she ran toward the scene. When she got to our yard, I grabbed onto her and held tightly. The EMTs were preparing to move Butch onto a backboard for transport, so I rushed into the house to grab the necessary insurance cards, my purse, a sweater, and a phone charger. Even in my fear and my disbelief at what had happened, I was amazed that I was clear-headed enough to grab all of these things. I didn't see the crew load Butch onto the backboard and into the ambulance, but Tiffany did. Later she told me that what she saw convinced her there was no way Butch could survive. When they lifted him onto the backboard to carry him to the ambulance, Tiffany saw that the left side of Butch's chest was caved in. She didn't tell me what she saw, but she was obviously extremely upset. Tiffany said she thought, *Oh God, please don't make my mom go through this again.*

The ambulance pulled away, lights flashing and sirens screaming. Tiffany and I ran a half block down the street to her car past tons of neighbors watching with deep concern and headed toward the hospital. A fifteen-minute ride seemed to take days. Poor Logan was still in the back seat along with the family's border collie, Rudy. Even Rudy could sense something was very wrong. Logan was uncharacteristically quiet. He is an extremely intelligent, mature, sensitive young man and knew it was best not to ask questions yet. He saw the state I was in, heard me pray throughout the ride to the hospital, and sat in silence. I still don't know what was going through his mind.

When we arrived at the hospital, I fully expected to be taken immediately to where my husband was being treated but instead was held prisoner in the waiting room, denied permission to go back with him. Minutes ticked by. News of the accident traveled fast, so friends and family kept streaming into the waiting room. Some of the firemen from Butch's department as well as those who worked on him at our house were there. They were allowed in the emergency room next to the door of the unit where doctors were treating Butch. I called back and asked to be buzzed in, but the nurses wouldn't let me enter. Eventually the chief of the fire department came to give me a report. He was visibly shaken and chose his words carefully. He told me that my husband's ribs were broken and that his lung was punctured and collapsed. Doctors were working to stabilize him. The chief returned to the emergency room, and I stood there, staring at those double doors, knowing Butch was somewhere on the other side, in pain, in danger, and they wouldn't let me be with him. It was torture.

While I stood there, staring, shaking, trying to hold myself together, my mom called me from her room at Barnes Hospital. *Oh no! Mom!* I thought. She was supposed to be transported to a different rehab facility that day. I knew I had to answer, so I tried my best to make my voice sound as close to normal as possible. But moms aren't easily fooled. All I said was "Hello," and she responded, "What's wrong?" I said Butch had fallen off a ladder and was in the emergency room being examined by a doctor. That must have been enough to explain why my voice sounded full of concern, so she explained the purpose of her call. Hospital staff had told her she would be transported the next day to the rehabilitation facility, which was near our town. I told her that was great and I would see her tomorrow. Was it only the night before that we had visited her after attending the Cardinal game? This was less than twenty-four hours later. How could this be happening?

I've learned a lot about hospital waiting room culture. People tried to be polite but were naturally curious about why so many were there in support of one person. What had happened to him? People would look our way, averting their eyes if they met mine. The concern was evident on the faces of those who did not know us, but they didn't want to intrude or to appear impolite by asking questions. And those of us who were there, supporting one another, reacted differently to the same set of circumstances. Our grown children, family, friends, pastors, fire department comrades, and I responded to this crisis in varying ways.

This was a lonely, intimate, personal time. I looked at Joe and thought of his dad, my husband, who lost his own father when he was just twenty. Losing his dad so young was still difficult for Butch, even after thirty-nine years. I didn't want this for Joe. He was handling things well at this point because he was the oldest and it was his duty. His response also reflected his personality. Tiffany, the next oldest, was more like me. Butch was her stepfather, and she loved him. She was very upset but holding herself together. She and I react well during the acute phase of a crisis but have a meltdown long after it's over. Kristi, the next youngest, is Butch's baby girl. She doesn't often show emotion. Her attitude was that everything would be okay. There was no room in her for any other reaction. This was her daddy, and nothing could possibly happen to him. She was getting married in a few months, and he had to walk her down the aisle.

My ex-husband's wife, Melodie, was one of the first to arrive at the hospital. Butch's ex-wife's husband, Reda, was there too. There is a huge amount of history behind us that could be a whole book in itself, but the moral of all this is that God is good and that He is a redeemer. At times like this family is family, period. We all had been through so much together, so we had bonded years before, leaving any hurt or unforgiveness in the past. We hugged and waited. We prayed and waited. We cried and waited.

One of the firemen from Butch's department came through those horrible double doors to give me an update. He told me through tears that Butch was holding his own but that he would have to be taken by helicopter to Barnes Hospital in St. Louis. That was where my mom would be until she was moved the next day. I asked if doctors would let me see Butch, but the answer was still no. I didn't understand why. What could be so bad that they wouldn't let me back there?

We waited for what seemed to be hours. We heard the helicopter fly in and watched it land on the helipad across the road from the emergency room. We saw a security team block the road both ways to keep people safely away from the helipad. Staff members sent word that the helicopter couldn't fly out until the storm subsided and conditions were safe. I was to be ready, choose one person to accompany me, and when it was time we would have to hurry to see Butch. We would be allowed to stand in the hallway and speak to him as he was rushed to the helipad. There would be no time to stop with him; the encounter would be very brief. About fifteen minutes after the helicopter landed, word came for me and my person of choice, Joe, to head back to where Butch was. The crew was ready to rush him to the helicopter.

When we walked through those double doors that had separated me from my husband for so long, what I saw took my breath away. Straight across from the two doors was the door to my husband's trauma treatment room. The firemen were lined up at the door and ushered Joe and me to the threshold of the room. We could see Butch's feet. They began to wheel him out of the room, and the sight grabbed my heart like a vise. Chest tubes, IVs, machines, bandages, and monitors seemed to cover his body. I told him that I loved him and that we were following in the car and would be at Barnes as soon as we could. He laboriously produced the words "Be careful," and crew members whisked him away.

They rushed him across the road, loaded him into the helicopter, and took off. As the chopper rose, I thought this could very well be the last time I saw my husband alive. Melodie was standing next to me and took a picture of the takeoff. Butch's best friend Harry did the same. I had no desire for that picture, but Melodie's words made me feel a little guilty about my lack of faith. She said, "As a first responder himself, he's going to want to have a copy of this picture one day." Still, I had an uneasy, queasy feeling in the pit of my stomach. It was a nearly disabling fear.

Most of the people in the waiting room planned to go straight to Barnes. Why Tiffany and I wound up in the same car by ourselves I'll never understand. None of us were thinking clearly. The two of us were so upset that neither of us should have been behind the wheel. We sent Logan and the dog home with Melodie, who offered to take care of them, and headed toward Barnes Hospital—or so we thought. For some reason we took the wrong way into Missouri and had to backtrack, losing valuable minutes. The sky looked dark and dreary, and it was still raining. The weather mirrored how I felt. The natural and the figurative storms were churning, blowing, and thundering. Everything was out of my control. My husband was in a helicopter on his way to Barnes Hospital, and I didn't know if he would survive the trip. My mom was in the same hospital with end-stage COPD. She counted the number of helicopters that landed on the roof with critically injured patients. She didn't know that one of those helicopters was carrying her critically injured son-in-law. How was I going to do this? I felt like my head was spinning and I was going to be sick.

If it seemed to take days to reach the first hospital, it seemed to take an eternity to get to Barnes. The unknown can be paralyzing. I didn't know if we would make it in time. I didn't know if Butch would survive the flight. I wasn't sure if we were going in the right direction. About five minutes away from the hospital, I received a phone call from a dear friend who was in the emergency room at Barnes, waiting for us. He was concerned that we hadn't arrived. He said we could drive right up to the door and he would take the car to the parking garage. I hadn't even thought about parking. When we arrived, Tyler (who had started the Flat Butch shenanigans) took the car, and we rushed into the emergency room where we found many relatives and friends awaiting us.

Because of its location, the hospital has security similar to what you would encounter at an airport entrance. The process was laborious. All I wanted to do was to see my husband. I hoped he was back there somewhere, still trying to breathe. Once we all got through security, a guard approached me and said there was a special waiting room for us down the hall. This couldn't be a good sign. The waiting room was pretty full, but this sent up red flags for me. The emergency room personnel at one of the best hospitals in the country, where critically injured and gravely ill people were flown in from all over, had designated a special waiting room for the family and friends of Clyde "Butch" McGill? Oh, no.

Staffers escorted us down the hall to our private waiting room and said two people could go back to see Butch in a minute. Finally, confirmation that he at least survived the flight. Kristi and I were taken to the end of the hall, where Butch was being treated. He was on an emergency-room gurney-bed, one of those that aren't made for long-term comfort. He had an oxygen mask on his face. His eyes were open and he was trying to talk. I still didn't know anything beyond what I was told by the firemen at the first hospital. Butch kept trying to tell me it was hard to breathe. I assured him hospital personnel were aware of this and were doing everything they could to help him. He didn't know what had happened and kept asking me where he was and why he was there. I explained that he had fallen off the ladder and had broken ribs and a collapsed lung, which was why it was hard to breathe.

Butch seemed to be somewhat stable, and I suddenly realized that I had to go to the bathroom, so I told him I would be right back. I headed down the hall and sent Joe back to be with his dad and Kristi. I stepped into the bathroom, which was right by our private waiting room. Everything looked surreal. The walls seemed to have waves in them, and the floor was spinning. I took care of business, washed my hands, and walked out the door. Butch's ex-wife, Tammy, grabbed me and pushed me back into the bathroom. She closed the door, embraced me, and called out to Jesus for Butch's healing. We cried together, hugged, prayed, and assured each other that everything would be okay. When we stepped out of the bathroom, a nurse told me that Butch had been rushed up to the surgical, trauma, and burn intensive care unit.

The nurse escorted me on a shortcut through what looked like the hospital catacombs to reach this special unit. Everyone else had to go the regular way—to the public elevators, the grand entrance lobby, and the next set of elevators to the floor. I was taken straight to the ICU waiting room. I learned that there were several intensive care units at Barnes Hospital. In this one, surgical procedures were performed right in the room. Patients suffering the worst trauma were sent to this unit.

The waiting room was enormous, with several cubicles sectioned off. I eventually learned this was done to provide privacy for families who were hurting, waiting, hoping, and sometimes grieving. Death was common in this ICU. There were small, medium, and large cubicles, all with chairs, recliners, and couches that could double as beds. There were several TVs, and a machine delivered free coffee twenty-four hours a day. The waiting room had its own set of restrooms so families wouldn't have to go too far when nature called. But the best part of this waiting room was an angel of mercy named Pat. I called her Miss Pat. We weren't there long before Miss Pat appeared with a stack of blankets, a smile, and a warm hug for all of us. She made us feel that she cared as much for Butch as we did. She was a special person with a special ministry in that difficult place.

I never counted the number of people who came to support us and to pray that night, but they filled a large part of the waiting room. It was around 9:30 p.m. when we settled into chairs, onto tables, and anywhere else we could find to sit and wait. It had been four hours since Butch fell. I couldn't understand why I again wasn't allowed to be with him. Another set of double doors separated us, and there was no way to get through them. Miss Pat kept going back to see if she could learn anything, but she always returned with the same message: hospital personnel would come get me when they had Butch settled and stable. We waited. And waited. And waited.

Though many people were there—family, friends, and pastors—I felt completely isolated. Nothing could relieve my panic. I trusted God. I knew He was in control. I also knew that sometimes He allows bad things to happen for reasons we cannot understand. I'd experienced this in the past, and I knew it was possible that it could happen again. I didn't lack faith. So I prayed. Miss Pat sat with me and prayed. Everyone took turns sitting with me and praying. I kept saying that I couldn't believe this had happened and that I didn't understand why I couldn't see my husband. I stared at those double doors. Everyone wore a worried look. Something didn't feel right.

We waited for close to five hours before the family could see Butch. Doctors were running an enormous number of tests because he had multiple injuries. I didn't know what the injuries were, but at one point Miss Pat told me tests were being done on his heart.

27

His heart? What was wrong with his heart? When we were allowed through the double doors, we saw an enormous ICU unit like none I'd ever seen. It was basically the full length of the hospital on one side and half the length on the other. Butch's room was at the end of the longest part of the unit.

When we entered his room, he was awake. I had to work to hold back the tears, partly because I was relieved to see him alive and partly because of how he looked. His bed was in a full upright position to help him breathe. Butch had a central line inserted on his left clavicle area, oxygen on his face, several IVs, two chest tubes, a neck brace, a bandage on his right arm, and scrapes and bruises on the side of his head; he was struggling to breathe. He was glad to see all of us and commented as best he could about how wonderful the doctors and the nurses had been to him. He asked us to be sure to thank them all for being so kind. Then he said how much he loved each of us, which was a little troubling. It was as if he were saying good-bye.

One of his many doctors finally came to talk to us about Butch's injuries. It was now around 3:00 a.m., about nine-and-a-half hours after he fell off the ladder. Several of his ribs were broken, perhaps all of them, and he had suffered tension hemopneumothorax, a collapsed lung that released air and blood into the chest cavity, significantly displacing the heart and major vessels to the right. He had also suffered subarachnoid brain bleed, soft tissue damage to the neck that could cause paralysis, a compression fracture to the sixth thoracic vertebrae, several fractured transverse processes of the thoracic vertebrae, suspected breaks to both wrists, scrapes, bruises, and abrasions. Butch was in trouble but was in the best possible hands. As we learned later, what made this so much worse was that, when inserting the first chest tube to reinflate Butch's lung, a doctor at the first hospital accidentally punctured the lung, just missing the aorta, resulting in the need for a second chest tube. This would soon create many more problems.

The prognosis was that if Butch made it through the night, he would need surgery the next day to remove the misplaced chest tube. He was stable for the moment, so the doctor recommended that everyone try to get some rest. I encouraged everyone to go home and sleep for a while, but I was not going to leave my husband now that I was finally able to be by his side. The rooms in the ICU unit were enormous, and most were equipped with at least a recliner for a family member to stay with the patient. The recliners were poorly designed. They were great for sitting or slightly reclining, but when I tried to settle back all the way to get some sleep, the recliner would pop back halfway, folding me up like a taco. I couldn't sleep anyway, but getting my body to relax would have been a relief. Butch didn't get much chance to rest either. Orthopedic specialists came in to X-ray his right wrist and found a severe break. The wrist had to be set as a temporary measure so that when he was stable enough, they could perform surgery to piece it back together.

Setting a badly shattered wrist is not a pleasant thing to watch, much less to experience. First, the doctor injected anesthetic into Butch's wrist, which was obviously painful. My poor husband was struggling to breathe and was completely exhausted from his ordeal. He had enough energy only to grunt a little when injected with the needle. After the injection, the doctor inserted Butch's fingers into a contraption that reminded me of the Chinese finger traps that we used to get at school carnivals. You pushed your fingers in, and they were held tightly in a flexible little tube when you tried to pull them out. Butch's four fingers were secured in this contraption, which was hung from an IV pole. Then a weight was hung from his bicep to stretch his wrist, separating the bones enough to be repositioned as close to the correct placement as possible.

About twenty minutes after this procedure, the doctor returned to the room and said, "Mr. McGill, this is going to hurt but only for about fifteen seconds." When the doctor manipulated the bones in the wrist, Butch didn't even flinch or open his eyes. I don't know if it was exhaustion or the grace of God, but I was relieved that he didn't seem to suffer through this. The doctor splinted and bandaged Butch's right hand up to above the elbow and said this would at least keep the wrist stable until it could be surgically repaired.

The next hour or two was quiet, but doctors were in and out constantly. First thing in the morning, a pulmonary specialist talked to me about the badly misplaced chest tube and what needed to be done. Butch would have to have surgery later that day, Tuesday, to remove it. This had to be done in the operating room because when the tube was removed, extreme bleeding or damage to the lung could result. He described the possible scenarios. One was that doctors could pull the tube and Butch's body would seal itself as the tube came out. This was the best scenario. Another possibility was that there would be a lot of bleeding, and doctors would have to open him up and repair the damage. The third and worst possibility was that the lung would be so damaged from the badly placed tube that they would be forced to remove part or all of his lung. I was to stay close during the surgery so they could find me to sign consent if this procedure was necessary. The doctor also explained that no matter the scenario, Butch would be placed on a ventilator for some time after the surgery and that I shouldn't be concerned. He said this would make Butch more comfortable and would help his lungs to heal. He would be sedated but would most likely be able to communicate by blinking his eyes or through facial expressions. Surgery was scheduled for 3:30 that afternoon.

Tuesday, July 8

At 6:00 a.m. and 6:00 p.m., visitors to the ICU were required to leave the patient rooms for two hours so the shift change and patient assessments could be done without interference. I assumed everyone had gone home to get a few hours of sleep, but when I entered the waiting room I found Butch's best friend, Harry, asleep in one of the chairs. It was such a relief to see him. He awoke as soon as I walked into the cubicle he was occupying. He told me he wasn't going home until he knew Butch would be okay. I told him Butch was holding his own and filled him in about the surgery later that day.

Harry decided to go down to the cafeteria to get something to eat and offered to bring back something for me. I asked for hot cereal and coffee. When he returned with my food, it was impossible for me to choke down more than a few bites. We tried to talk, but the weight of worry on both of us made it difficult. In addition to my husband's crisis, this was also the day my mother was to be transported across the river to a rehabilitation facility. I hadn't talked to her since she called me the evening before. What was I going to do? She was only a few floors away, but I couldn't go up to see her. I couldn't leave the waiting room for fear that something would happen. My cell phone reception was terrible in the hospital. Only one carrier had a good signal, and it wasn't mine. I felt pulled between my mom and my husband, totally helpless in both situations.

Later that morning, after I was allowed back into Butch's room, one of the pulmonary surgeons who was going to be in the operating room spoke to me. We were discussing the procedure and possible complications when she carefully suggested that I consider praying. She didn't know me, so she was unaware of my relationship with God. I told her I had been praying, as had our family and friends, and that I knew the Great Physician was in control. With that she said, "Now that I know where you stand, let's call on the name of Jesus to guide and direct us in that operating room!" She called on the Holy Spirit to fill Butch's room right then. Wow. It was incredible to know that my husband was in this woman's hands. She was part of a team of surgeons who would be in the operating room. I trusted that God would guide them.

The rest of the morning and the early afternoon were filled with visits from doctors. The head of trauma surgery. The head of cardio-thoracic surgery. The head of orthopedics. The head of neurology. The attending ICU doctor. Several residents and interns. Respiratory therapists. Nurses. Technicians. At some point I managed to mention to someone the dilemma brewing with my mom. One of them suggested I ask if the hospital would consider keeping my mom for at least a few more days so I could focus on my husband and still be close to her.

Butch was resting and seemed stable and Harry was there, so I slipped upstairs to see my mom. She was a mess and cried when she saw me. I couldn't hide anything from my mom, but I didn't tell her how bad things were with Butch. I tried to blame my frazzled appearance on lack of sleep. I'm not sure she bought my explanation, but she didn't push too hard for information. I told her about Butch's impending surgery and said I would return to see her after it was over to let her know how he was doing. I gave her a hug and left the room, choking back the tears. How much can one person handle? When I got to the nurses' station on Mom's floor, I asked to speak to the attending physician. She was close by, so I didn't have to wait. I explained the situation and the doctor looked at me in disbelief. This was a unique situation, even for the people at Barnes Hospital, who had seen just about everything. The doctor said that she would do what she could to help me but that the insurance company and Medicare would ultimately make the decision for us. I thanked her and headed back to the ICU.

It was time to prepare Butch for surgery. Moving a patient in his condition was no easy task. The portable monitors, IVs, and oxygen took up so much room on the bed that there was barely room for Butch. It took twenty to thirty minutes to load everything and to make sure that it was all working properly and that he was stable. I remember that Joe, Kristi, Jeff, Tiffany, Jeremy, and Harry were there. If there were others, I was too exhausted and overwhelmed to remember them. While Butch was in the pre-op holding area, only Joe, Kristi, and I were allowed to sit with him. He was still struggling to breathe, and it was getting increasingly difficult to watch. By this time I found it next to impossible to stop crying. I didn't want Butch to see me cry. I was trying to be strong for him to show him that I was okay and that he would be okay. I reached up and kissed him on the lips. He tried to kiss me back, but it was hard to kiss when he couldn't breathe.

Butch was still wearing a neck brace, which was irritating him. Staffers would not remove it until he could tell them that his neck did not hurt. The brace presented a problem for the intubation required for the surgery. The anesthesiologist and the neurosurgeon carefully removed the collar to see if he had pain. Since his scans showed no structural damage to his vertebrae or spinal cord, they felt it safe to ask him to move his head so they could assess for pain. Butch tried to turn his head a little to the left and indicated that this hurt. The collar went back on, and the anesthesiologist had to negotiate intubating him with this obstacle. We prayed for this man. A team of anesthesiologists and doctors formed a circle and prayed before the surgery.

A few minutes later, they came to take Butch to surgery. I kissed him on the forehead and told him I loved him, and he was gone. Again, I felt that this could be the last time I saw my husband alive. A nurse escorted us back to the waiting room. As I walked down the hallway between the pre-op area and the waiting room, my knees buckled. I guess the emotion, fear, exhaustion, and trauma of the past twenty-four hours had taken a toll on my body. Joe must have been watching me closely, because he was right there to catch me, keeping me from falling to the floor. He supported me for the rest of the walk to the waiting room. I was so thankful that he was there.

We sat quietly in the waiting room, all of us emotional and exhausted. I kept thinking about what the doctor had told me earlier that day—that Butch could lose a lung. I knew that people could live with only one lung, but to my mind that was not the same as living with one kidney. If the only kidney you have fails, dialysis can keep you alive until an alternative is found. If the only lung you have fails, what then? I prayed. By now I had prayed so much that I didn't know what to say. But the beauty of our loving God is that He already knows what we need. I knew that all I had to do was ask God to take control and He would. I'd like to say that my faith allowed me to relax and to have total peace, but the truth is I was terrified. I was afraid I would lose my husband, and I wasn't sure I could handle that. I knew that sometime in the next few minutes or hours, a doctor would tell me the outcome of the surgery. Until then, my human nature would rule. I knew the Bible said not to worry. But I worried—and prayed and cried.

About two hours after Butch was taken into surgery, the receptionist at the desk in the surgical waiting room paged me to the phone. This might be a good thing, since no one had come to ask for my permission to remove his lung. I picked up the receiver and heard a cheerful voice say, "Hi, Mrs. McGill. This is Doctor _____. We were able to remove the tube without any complication. His lung sealed with minimal bleeding. He'll be back in his room in about an hour." I started to cry, which my family interpreted as bad news. I quickly assured everyone that it was the best possible news and that our prayers had been answered. What a relief! I thought that we were over the hump and that Butch would begin to heal and quickly get stronger. I even thought we might be able to go on our vacation, which started that Friday. Of course Butch would have to take it easy, and we'd have to sit on the beach and rest, allowing him to recuperate. It's amazing how exhaustion can cloud the thinking process. Even if nothing else went wrong, Butch would never be able to tolerate the fourteen-hour ride to Hilton Head Island. And we didn't know that he wasn't out of the woods yet—not even close.

When Butch was finally taken back to his room in the ICU, he was semi-awake. He seemed comfortable, and the promised ventilator was humming away, breathing for him. He had two chest tubes coming from his left side. Including the badly misplaced one, that was a total of three since the accident. Finally, twenty-four hours after the accident, Butch wasn't struggling to breathe. Though it was scary seeing my beloved husband with a tube down his throat connected to a noisy machine, I had peace knowing that this set-up was keeping him alive. I tenderly approached the right side of the bed, gently kissed him on the forehead, and assured him that the surgery went as well as it possibly could have gone. Butch clearly wasn't completely aware of what had happened to him, but he blinked his eyes, signaling he understood. He was obviously relieved to see me and Joe, who stood on the other side of the bed. I tried to update Butch on who had been to the hospital, who had sent messages of support and prayer, and who was offering to take care of our house and our yard. I wanted to assure him that things were in good hands and that he didn't need to worry about anything except getting better.

Even amid exhaustion, fear, and anxiety, humor can surprise us, offering brief relief from emotional intensity. I was explaining how our friend Tyler, of Flat Butch fame, was helping us. Tyler and his wife were owners of a brand-new funeral home. Butch worked for them part time, opening doors during services. We had purchased an empty lot next to their new home and were planning to build our new house within the next few months. When I was listing those who had offered their help, I told Butch that Tyler was taking care of arrangements. This elicited quite a response from my husband. It's incredible how someone can communicate with eyebrows and eyelids. I was explaining that Tyler was making sure our lot was mowed, but Butch interpreted the word *arrangements* as involving Tyler's profession. Oh, those eyebrows spoke volumes. I quickly explained what I meant and said that Tyler was not arranging his funeral but a mowing schedule. Though Butch's injuries and his condition were extremely critical, Joe and I laughed—hard. I'm not sure Butch thought this was funny, but fortunately one of the sedation medications being pumped into his veins caused him to forget much of what was happening. So even though he was briefly concerned, he didn't remember the incident. But Joe and I remembered. It was a small gift, a release of pent-up emotion that helped us to relax just a little.

The rest of Tuesday night went fairly smoothly. Butch was sedated and breathing with the help of the ventilator, and things were quiet for the moment.

CHAPTER 4

Wednesday, July 9

Doctors raised the possibility of extubating Butch that day or early Thursday but couldn't agree on his case. They also discussed giving him an epidural for pain control because when they lowered the sedation he felt the pain from his injuries. However, his platelets were low, creating a dangerous situation for an epidural. Butch could bleed into the spinal cord, which could cause paralysis. Doctors opted not to do the epidural. They made it clear that he would experience excruciating pain when he awoke. Most or all of his ribs were broken, which would make it difficult to take deep breaths. His left lung had suffered extreme injury from the fall and from the chest tube that had punctured it. By this time doctors had discovered that his left wrist as well as his right wrist was broken. Butch had a brain injury and a compression fracture in his T6 vertebrae. He was bruised and swollen. Doctors were trying to find the best way to manage all this before they extubated Butch so he could breathe deeply enough to fight pneumonia. Because they couldn't agree on how to proceed, they kept him on the ventilator.

No decision was made on Wednesday. We settled in late that night after all relatives and friends had left. The room was quiet, and I now had an amazing couch, which a wonderful young woman named Amy brought for me. It fit neatly behind the head of Butch's bed next to a huge window overlooking Forest Park—the same park

I had viewed from my mom's window a few floors up. We had visited her after that Cardinal game only three days before—a lifetime ago, it seemed.

Family and friends from all over the country were active on Facebook, so news of Butch's accident had traveled quickly and there were frequent posts about what was happening. After the accident I initially had zero interest in looking at Facebook, let alone posting. However, a lot of incorrect information and speculation had been shared, so I decided that I would post updates as often as I could, providing accurate information about Butch's condition and progress. I had no idea how many people would eventually follow these posts. This happened not only because they wanted to keep up to date about Butch but because God was doing something incredible throughout this ordeal, speaking through my posts to everyone reading them. God can be creative. He loves us so much and will use any means to communicate this to us. I began most posts as updates introduced by day, date, and time. I did this so I could easily find these posts and set them apart from other posts on my timeline. From this point on, much of what you will read will be messages that I posted in real time on Facebook. I want to share the posts to recreate events. These posts are indented in block form for easy recognition.

Though Wednesday evening was fairly calm, another huge storm was looming on the horizon, and I had no idea what was about to blow into Butch's room.

> **Update: 9:30 p.m.** Butch is resting quietly. He is running a fever, but this is not unexpected. Doctors have pretty much nixed the epidural at this point. It is too dangerous because with the platelet count going low, he could bleed into his spinal cord, risking very bad things. For now, they will try to manage the pain with alternate methods.

Mom appears to have a urinary tract infection, which is causing her to be pretty miserable. It's so torturous for her to be upstairs and unable to comfort her daughter. I feel so bad for her. We believe this is why she is having the panic attacks.

I hope you all don't get tired of the updates. God is so good. I can feel him carrying me—us. I wish my natural eyes could see into the spirit realm. I believe a battle is raging for Butch McGill. Please keep praying.

The only good thing about my mom's urinary tract infection was that this meant she would stay in the hospital for at least another day.

Amy, a longtime friend of ours, had been fighting a battle of her own for years. When her daughter was only a few months old, she was diagnosed with a rare form of brain cancer. The doctors offered no hope and asked if they could use an experimental treatment on the baby girl, making her a guinea pig. Her parents said an emphatic no and began storming heaven on her behalf, assisted by hundreds of us who joined in the battle. Deborah is a miracle. She is now in elementary school and has a special connection with God. This is a post on a conversation and prayer time that Amy and Deborah had about Butch.

Wednesday, July 9: Amy writes, "Deborah's prayer tonight: 'Thank you, Jesus, for Butch, and thank you, Jesus, that he will feel better soon. Thank you, Jesus, for hospitals and nurses and even IVs because they make us better. Thank you, Jesus, for his mom … (She opens her eyes.) Mom, what are you to Daddy?' Me: 'Wife.' Deb: 'Thank you, Jesus, for his wife, and thank you, Jesus, for her staying with him. Thank you, Jesus, for Logan [our grandson] that he can be a good boy to them. Thank you, Jesus, that you will make Butch all better as soon as you want to. Thank you, Jesus, for all the miracles that you do for others, even for me. Amen.'"

I cannot read this without tearing up. Such maturity in a little girl who has been through way too much in her short life. But this little one is a powerful prayer warrior. She knows where our help comes from.

Thursday, July 10

> **Update: 6:15 a.m.** Call to all prayer warriors: Butch is in trouble. Pray.

> **Update: 6:31 a.m.** I can post this only once to everyone. I don't know what is happening. Butch started shaking very hard and seems to be in severe respiratory distress. He is already on a ventilator. I'm in here with him with all the docs. They are trying to figure it out.

The following is not a Facebook post but a narrative describing events on what I call Bad Thursday.

2:00 a.m., Surgical, Trauma, and Burn Intensive Care Unit at Barnes Hospital: The ICU resident entered the room and said that doctors planned to try to extubate sometime within the next hour. I was very concerned and so was Butch's nurse. She said there were not enough personnel available at night to cover an emergency, so this was dangerous in her eyes. Though my husband had passed a breathing trial, I had an uneasy feeling. I couldn't discount the nurse's hesitation to do this procedure in the middle of the night with a skeleton crew on the floor. Something felt off. Thankfully, the issue was resolved when the staff became busy with another patient and postponed an attempt to remove Butch from the ventilator for a few hours.

6:00 a.m. The doctor turned the propofol way down, attempting to bring Butch out of sedation. The doctor also turned the ventilator way down to observe Butch's ability to breathe on his own. The instant he dialed down the ventilator, my husband went into crisis. The nurse thought he was "freaking out" (her words) because the sedation was wearing off. She tried to calm Butch, reassuring him that he was okay and telling him to breathe. In fact, his life was in danger. The monitors beeped and chirped, signaling that his vital signs were dropping quickly. He began to convulse, his body shaking violently.

6:15 a.m. Arriving for her shift, the attending doctor on the floor walked past Butch's room as he was convulsing. She ran in and took charge. A whole team followed—doctors, nurses, respiratory therapists, and others. They didn't waste time asking me to leave, because the situation was so critical. Right in front of me they sliced Butch's right side and inserted yet another chest tube, the fourth one. Blood was everywhere on the floor. Next they ran a scope down his throat to see what was happening in his lungs. Then everything turned upside down. I stood at the head of his bed, watching helplessly, and cried out to God.

As soon as I could, I called Joe. My daughter-in-law, Kelli, answered the phone. She told me that Joe was in the shower but that he was planning to come to the hospital. I explained what was happening and asked her to have him hurry. People quickly started arriving at the hospital. This was the type of situation where the family was called. I didn't do that, but my post was enough to communicate the gravity of the situation. Doctors were trying to stabilize Butch enough to take him for a CT scan to try to determine what was going on. When they inserted the scope into his lungs, we all could see that when he inhaled, his bronchial tubes would open, allowing air to enter. When he exhaled, fluid would flow from the left side to the right, causing the bronchial tubes to close to protect the lung. Wait. Was fluid supposed to be flowing between the bronchial tubes? I had gone to nursing school. I understood a great deal about anatomy, and I knew this was not supposed to be happening. The doctor in charge was talking through the problem out loud, trying to figure out this mystery. Butch's life depended on a quick answer.

We were escorted to that special waiting room where no one wanted to be— the waiting room sequestered from the main waiting room; the waiting room where hospital workers brought coffee and cookies because that's what they did when a family was about to get bad news; the waiting room with a door that could be closed for privacy. I didn't want to leave Butch. Once again, I feared that I had seen him alive for the last time. I could barely sit. I could barely stand. The room filled with people. I needed a box of tissues because by now the tears would not stop flowing. The nurse who had cared for Butch throughout the night, the one who was hesitant to remove the ventilator in the early hours of the morning, had finished her shift but stayed to sit with us. She was visibly upset.

After what seemed to be hours, the doctor who rushed in when Butch was convulsing came to talk to us. She asked us to walk with her to the computer terminal immediately outside of Butch's room. All of the rooms in the ICU had computer stations directly outside. Medical personnel could enter information at these stations while keeping eyes on the patients. Doctors also took several portable computer stations with them while doing rounds on the floor. As we walked to the computer station, Kelli told me that Joe had said to her the night before that he had decided the best thing he could do for his dad was to take care of me. He had made it his responsibility to see that I was okay. I was floored that even while watching his dad fight for his life during an unbelievable ordeal, Joe was thinking about my welfare. He's a lot like his father.

When we got to the computer terminal, Doctor T pulled up images on the screen and showed us a comparison between the CT scan of Butch's lungs from Monday night and the scan just taken. Though I had medical training, it didn't take any special knowledge to understand what we saw. The first image showed a milky-looking left lung but a fairly clear right lung. The scan from that day showed two very cloudy lungs. Doctor T looked me in the eye and said, "We don't know why, but now his right lung is schmutzed." I hated the choice of words. I thought, *How in the world can he survive with both lungs full of fluid and damaged?* I looked desperately at Joe and could see the concern on his face.

We returned to the sad waiting room. Doctor T came in a little later, knelt beside me, and explained what was going on. She said the good thing about being at Barnes Hospital was that a lot of smart people at the top of their field were collaborating on Butch's case. Then she said the bad thing was that these smart people couldn't agree on the best course of action. This did not help me to relax. Essentially doctors had discovered that in the area where the chest tube had punctured Butch's left lung, a pocket of infection had developed. That pocket had filled with fluid and was communicating the fluid to his good lung. The team disagreed over how to handle this. One doctor wanted to insert a drain to pull the fluid out of the pocket, removing the threat to the right lung. This option could result in the need for surgery later to repair the damage done by the drain, but that was something the team could handle. Another doctor wanted to leave the infection alone, keep Butch on life support, and let his body handle the problem. However, if the infection advanced to a certain point, there would be nothing doctors could do and he would die. Though I had only attended nursing school and didn't finish because God had called me back into teaching, the decision seemed clear. I wanted them to insert the drain, and fast.

By the time Doctor T had finished explaining the situation, Butch had stabilized enough so that we could breathe a little easier and no longer had to be kept in the waiting room reserved for people who might receive bad news. We moved into the large waiting room and occupied the biggest cubicle, which had two couches and several chairs. We settled in for what promised to be a long, emotional day.

I had not had much to eat or drink since that Monday afternoon when I sat at our kitchen table and had a sandwich before heading out to power-wash the deck. I hadn't slept either. People were encouraging me to eat and drink, but my body rejected almost everything I put in my mouth. I tried to drink water, but even that made my stomach churn. I was surrounded by family and friends but felt isolated and alone. People tried to help me feel better. The hospital chaplain and I had become well acquainted, and Miss Pat had learned all of our first names. Many of our friends brought in food for the wait. Finally, sometime that evening, the doctor who won the debate about how to treat my husband came to talk to me in the waiting room. He told me his colleagues had finally agreed to go with his plan, which was to insert the drain. *Thank you, Lord*, I thought. He said, "I'll get him through this." I asked him to promise me, and he said, "I can't make any promises." Then he rushed off to take care of my husband.

Butch's daughter Kristi and her fiancé Jeff were sitting near our pastor in the waiting room. Their wedding was planned for November 8. Kristi said that if her dad didn't make it, she wasn't going to have a wedding, that they would get married at the courthouse because a ceremony would be too painful without her daddy. At that point, our pastor stood up and said, "Hey, let's go in Butch's room right now, and I'll marry you!" We all had a little laugh, but the reality was that we had no idea what would happen. For now, though, Butch seemed to be holding his own, so we decided we'd wait on the pastor's offer and pray for Butch's healing.

Update: July 10: Prayer warriors, you are amazing. Thank you. For now, Butch is stable. Several things happened today that I can hardly even describe.

All of them surprised every doctor on his case. In a nutshell, his good lung (right) is pretty sick with pneumonia. There is infection in the left lung in an air pocket and a fistula (hole) between both lungs. The left lung's infection is "communicating" with the right lung via the fistula. (We received more correct info on this later). To keep this from getting worse, they are going to put a drain in the left-lung fluid pocket. This is necessary but also can create a scenario for more problems. They also believe that not only has he broken every rib on the left side but several on the right as well.

The deal is that within the time frame since the accident, things still can pop up that didn't originally show. Hopefully now we are passing that seventy-two-hour mark where, if we can get Butch through this, he should turn a corner.

Specific prayer requests: that the fistula will close naturally and soon; that the infection will respond very quickly to the antibiotics; that his lungs will heal very quickly, enabling him to get off the ventilator; that they will be able to control his pain.

Thank you all. There is a battle raging right now, and we need all prayer warriors to storm heaven on his behalf. It's working.

Update: 6:04 p.m. They've taken Butch down to insert the drain into his left lung. My previous post had some incorrect information. There is not a fistula between the lungs. It is in his left lung. This isn't the real problem right now. Fluid is traveling

from a fluid-filled sac in his left lung to his right
lung via the natural pathway through the bronchial
tubes. They are draining the sac to stop this process.
The result will be another fistula created by the
drain, which may need surgical intervention later.
Please continue to pray. His clinical picture looks
better this evening than this morning. We need to
keep going in this direction.

The surgery went well. Butch now had two chest tubes and a
drain in his left side and another chest tube on his right. He was
still on the ventilator, had both hands, wrists, and arms splinted
and bandaged, wore a neck brace, and had a central line delivering
all of the medications needed to sustain life and keep him sedated.
Monitors surrounded him. I learned to depend on those monitors.
They chirped and screamed when things were off, and that meant
help would be on the way quickly if needed. As midnight approached,
everyone had gone home, and I settled into my little area with
the couch, which I now lovingly called "my cubby." The nurses
supplied me with pillows and warm blankets, making it clear that
my presence in Butch's room was welcomed and helpful. I was glad
because even if there were no couch or recliner, I would have stayed
in that room with him.

> **Update: 11:33 p.m**. Powerful. The youth camp
> at Carlinville is storming heaven on Butch's
> behalf. This is what it's all about. Thank you, Eric
> Hoffman, and everyone involved and all who have
> been praying. This is why we still have Butch.

> **Update: 11:40 p.m**. This day has been such a roller
> coaster. I will try to be brief, but first I want to say
> thank you to everyone who dropped everything to
> come and support us today. There aren't words to

explain how grateful and humbled I am. Some of you will understand this: I have a bottle of water beside me right now and I'm drinking some.

Our day started off in such a terrible way that without the intervention of God and doctors, the outcome would have been unthinkable. I won't go into detail, because most of you have read something about it through the day. Just know that we are truly blessed.

Tonight, as I lie quietly on the couch in my "apartment" (a cubbyhole behind Butch's bed), I am reflecting on this week. I have seen the hand of God work so many times in so many ways. I found out tonight that the chain saw Butch was using fell on top of him, landing on his chest. From fifteen feet. And he survived. Because of God ...

He is stable tonight. They have him heavily sedated and will keep him that way at least until tomorrow evening. He is still on a ventilator, and thank God he is. If they had extubated last night ...

Tonight is peaceful. He is moving in the right direction. It's because of all of you praying. There is a battle raging for Butch McGill. Keep praying, please!

One more thing: if any of you come to see him tomorrow, don't panic if you get to his room and it is vacated. ICU has quite a few empty rooms on this end, and for patient safety they will be moving us up the hall sometime during the night.

Have a blessed night. I can't wait for him to start sharing this testimony.

Friday, July 11

On this morning, a nurse we hadn't seen was assigned to Butch for the day shift. Her name was Maggie, and she was a beautiful young lady with a lot of energy. She was clearly on top of everything. Maggie soon told me she was moving Butch to a room closer to the center of the unit, right by the main nurses' station. My only request was that there be a couch for me in that room, and Maggie made sure that would happen. Our new room was directly across from the nurses' station, and I could see everything happening there. It was obvious to me why Maggie made this move. She told me it was "safer" to be at this location. I knew this meant that Butch was in extremely critical condition and in an emergency needed to be as close to where most personnel would be. She didn't say it and I didn't ask her, but it was understood where we were—still not out of the woods.

> **Update: 5:00 a.m.** An uneventful, uninterrupted night. I got about five hours of sleep, which feels like months. I'm not sure I moved the whole night. They are preparing to move Butch down the hall in the ICU to get us and our nurse closer to civilization. Many patients have left the ICU. This will make the walk to the bathroom about three-quarters of a mile instead of a whole mile. (I'm not sure I'm exaggerating.) The sun is about to rise on a day when I believe everything will be wonderful. Please keep praying.

Update: Tyler brought my mail to me last night in a bag. I just started to go through it. This was in the mail. Butch ordered it for me.

A T-shirt I asked Butch to order for me. It was delivered a few days after the accident.

A few weeks before, Butch and I had seen this shirt advertised on Facebook, and I mentioned that I wanted it. He ordered it for me. The timing of its arrival was perfect. I decided I would often wear that shirt until he woke up and would definitely wear it on the first day he was conscious.

Update: 9:28 a.m. They tried to lower his sedation a little, and that did not go well. He immediately started to labor in breathing. He will be kept in deep sedation for a while yet so he can heal. My concern is that the nurse told me today that Butch's condition will get worse before it gets better due to the progression of the bruising. Prayer warriors, again please help us do battle on his behalf. I can't imagine at this point what worse will look like.

This photo was taken Tuesday (July 8), honoring the man whose face is on the Flat Butch pictures and whose body is fighting in the ICU.

Pictured here are all of our kids and their spouses, our grandson Logan, and Tyler. Tiffany and Logan are on the left. Joe and Kelli are on the right in back. Tyler is next to Joe. Jeff, Kristi, and Jeremy are in the center. Everyone is holding a Flat Butch. This picture was taken after the surgery to remove the tube from Butch's lung and before Bad Thursday.

July 11: Mom update: My cousins rushed to my rescue yesterday and took Mom duty. I stayed away from her room all day because I didn't want her to see me looking like I did. They said she was smiling, eating a little, and generally in good spirits. Thank you, Lord.

Sometime that day, my phone rang. I knew by the caller ID that it was the manager of my mom's assisted living facility. I handed the phone to my cousin Barb, asking her to deal with this woman. I didn't have the strength to talk to her. I heard Barb say, "You do understand what's going on right now, correct? Her husband is fighting for his life right now in the ICU at Barnes Hospital. You're kidding, right?" This lady had told my cousin that since my mom had been away from her apartment for so long, we needed to pick up her belongings and surrender the apartment in the next couple of days. Really? Even though my whole family and most of our friends were camping out at the hospital, we were required to deal with this. If not for Tiffany and Jeremy, my cousins, and my friends, I have no idea how we would have managed.

Tiffany went that evening to start packing her beloved grandmother's things. She did this alone, so the work was emotionally too much for her. The week had been unbelievable, and now, on top of everything, she had this task because her grandmother was being booted out of her apartment. I understood that someone probably needed the apartment, but I had been told that as long as my mom was making progress and there was hope for her return, the apartment would be held for her. Though the doctors at Barnes kept giving me a dismal prognosis, I held on to the hope that she could return to her apartment. Now the plan was for family and friends to converge on my mom's apartment early Saturday morning, load trucks with her stuff, and move it to Kristi's basement. Kristi was living in the house where her grandmother, Butch's mom, had lived. When she passed away, Butch and I purchased the house, and we were now renting it to Kristi. Thankfully there was a place to take my mom's things, which included two rooms of furniture. Though her apartment was small, she had a lot of stuff.

As if things weren't complicated enough, later that day I was called to my mom's floor. Her doctor told me she was being prepared for transport to the rehabilitation facility across the river, in Illinois. The doctor said that nothing more could be done for Mom at the hospital and that the insurance company required the move. I was in shock. There had been no warning. I gathered myself, entered her room, and tried to be as cheerful as possible. The ambulance was already on its way to get her, so I didn't have much time to visit. In a nutshell, Butch was fighting for his life in the ICU, and in a few minutes my mom was being transported to a rehabilitation facility that I had never seen by ambulance drivers whom she had never met. She was going to a place where she knew no one, and no one was available to go with her or to meet her there to help her settle in. To make matters worse, even though all of this was happening, I was required by the manager of the assisted living facility to clean out her apartment. I was numb. The people around me were angry. I didn't have the strength to be angry. I just cried out to God for help.

While I was in the room with my precious mom, helping to pack the few belongings she had with her at the hospital, the paramedics arrived to transport her to the rehab facility. They were young men who treated her very well. They gently helped her onto the gurney and covered her with a blanket. I rode the elevator down with her to the exit where they would load her into the ambulance for the trip. As I stood there saying my good-byes, I noticed how weak and sad my mom looked. She was curled into a nearly fetal position. She wasn't a very big person. She used to stand five seven but in her later years had shrunk to around five three due to osteoporosis. She weighed a mere 115 pounds at most. I hugged and kissed her good-bye, assuring her that I would get over to see her as soon as I could. She told me that wasn't necessary and said my place was with Butch. As they loaded her into the ambulance, I thought this could be the last time I would see my mother alive. I went into the nearest bathroom, locked myself in the stall farthest from the door, and silently screamed for a long time.

After finishing my meltdown, I rinsed my face in the sink and tried to make myself presentable to head back upstairs to Butch's room. It was around 7:30 p.m. The image in the mirror looked nothing like I expected. I don't know why, but I thought I would look like, well, myself. Instead I saw a very tired, drawn, frazzled woman staring back at me. I had no time to worry about that, so I forgot about making myself presentable and headed back. However, at a place like Barnes Hospital, even though I looked pretty rough, many other people did as well. We were a family of strangers, and without speaking, we had an understanding of one another. I quickly adapted to this culture because it was my reality.

About two hours after my mom left the hospital, I received a phone call from a number I did not recognize. It was now around 8:30 p.m. on Friday. The caller identified herself as the charge nurse at the rehabilitation facility where my mom had been admitted only an hour before. She told me staffers were sending my precious mom to the emergency room because she was far too ill to be at their facility. She was running a fever and was extremely weak. My poor mom. Again, she was all alone, being taken by ambulance to the emergency room—the one where my husband was taken right after he fell. You can't make this stuff up. I was utterly helpless. I could only cry and pray. It was probably a good thing that Butch was unconscious at this time, because seeing me in this state would have been bad for him.

Now, in addition to everything else, I felt it was time to start thinking about what I would do if my mom passed away. With Butch in such precarious condition, a funeral would have been impossible. I called Tyler and asked his advice. My mom had a funeral prearrangement with him, so we had to look at our best option. Standing in the doorway of my husband's ICU room, I made verbal arrangements with Tyler to have my mom cremated if she died at that point. This would allow us to postpone funeral arrangements. My mom had always wished for this, but I had been hesitant. I found this too difficult to imagine for her, but now I saw no other option. Because I had her power of attorney for health care, I could make this decision without consulting my brothers. I asked their opinion anyway, and they supported my decision. Tyler said he would bring the paperwork, along with another load of mail from my house, to the hospital the next evening.

There was absolutely no way that I would have been able to make decisions for my mom and my husband or even to keep breathing if God hadn't carried me through these trials. And when I say that He carried me, I mean just that. By now I was low on food, fluids, and sleep, was facing the possible deaths of my husband and my mother, and had to arrange for her apartment to be cleared out immediately. I could not have handled all of this alone without falling apart. I was able to push on only because God carried me. He did this by sending the right person at the right time to help me. He spoke to me through that soft voice that many people understand and recognize. He sent exactly the right nurses and doctors to care for Butch. He gave people the right words to encourage me when I didn't think I could take another breath. He used music to comfort me. He spoke to me through a devotion book called *Jesus Calling* by Sarah Young. He sent people with just the right Scripture passages to share with me, assuring me He was in control of all of this. Through experience, I know that God is sovereign and that sometimes His ways aren't our ways. I had no choice but to trust Him.

Updates: July 11: Butch stable all morning and afternoon.

3:00 – Went to visit Mom on the twelfth floor of Queeny Towers (also Barnes) to find out they are transporting her today to Rosewood. They state they are not treating her for a medical problem. Made arrangements for transfer to happen at seven so I can stay with Butch until they kick everyone out of ICU for two hours.

5:00 – EKG for Butch. Heart issues due to lots of things. Nothing unexpected, but intervention needed. Meds given.

6:00 – Left ICU to be with Mom before transport. She looked miserable. Stayed with her until they picked her up.

7:30 – Walked with Mom and ambulance drivers as far as I could. Kissed and hugged her good-bye and sent her all by herself to Rosewood.

7:35 – Went to the bathroom and had a meltdown.

8:00 – Went into ICU with Butch to find them hustling to stabilize blood pressure because meds caused a drop. Nurses worked for over an hour to stabilize.

8:30 – Received a call that my mom is too sick to go to Rosewood. They are sending her back to the hospital. Called my cousin Carol, who has gone to manage the hospital admission.

8:40 – Meltdown number two.

9:00 – Butch fairly stable and quiet. Praise God.

10:30 – Carol called from Alton Memorial Hospital (AMH). Mom being admitted. Suspected pneumonia. Running hundred-degree fever. But she has no medical issues?

11:00 – The presence of God overwhelms me in my cubby. Butch's ventilator is becoming a soothing sound. It's rhythmic. It's him breathing.

CHAPTER 5

Saturday, July 12

Update: 5:55 a.m. After a very rough evening, God once again has made it evident that He is in control. His presence is so sweet, so intimate, and so powerful in Butch's room. I was warned that it would be a busy night, trying to get him balanced between heart rate and blood pressure. During all of this they are also lowering the oxygen coming through the ventilator, meaning they are weaning him off slowly. By 1:00 a.m., he quieted down and never had any more difficulties.

Around the same time, my mom was admitted to the intermediate care unit of the hospital with probable pneumonia. This means she is getting much more aggressive care for her condition.

And in my cubby, listening to the sweet hum of a ventilator supporting my incredible husband's breathing—allowing him more time to heal—I slept for another five hours.

Update: July 12: Psalm 34:1–9: "I bless God every chance I get; my lungs expand with his praise. I live and breathe God; if things aren't going well, hear this and be happy: join me in spreading the good news; together let's get the word out. God met me more than halfway; he freed me from my anxious fears. Look at Him; give Him your warmest smile. Never hide your feelings from Him. When I was desperate I called out, and God got me out of a tight spot. God's angels set up a circle of protection around us while we pray. Open your mouth and taste, open your eyes and see how good God is. Blessed are you who run to Him. Worship God if you want the best; worship opens doors to all His goodness."

Amen. The peace that passes all understanding surrounds me in my cubby. My mom is in the intermediate care unit at AMH, resting comfortably. Praise God. And I thank all of you who are continually praying. I can't believe all of this is happening. But I do believe that God is in control. Always.

A dear man and his wife from our church came to visit. When they stood beside Butch's bed, the man read this Scripture passage over Butch. As I said, God sent people with just the right words. When he read the phrase "my lungs expand with praise," my heart leapt. I took this to mean God was going to heal my husband.

Update: 1:26 p.m. Butch is having a rocky day. His fever has risen to 103 or so, and he is struggling a little. Today is a day that I really need to see a big improvement for me to be able to breathe.

Mom is in Alton Memorial on the intermediate care floor. She is in end-stage COPD. I know what this means. I'm just praying that the Lord waits awhile so I can be with my husband while he is fighting for his life.

Update: 8:01 p.m. Butch has been resting quietly today. I spoke to a doctor around five-thirty who said Butch is improving. And the Pitchfords brought me Bobby's.

July 12: (Tyler Pitchford's post) Bobby's has been delivered to the ICU waiting room. One of the biggest smiles we have seen on her this week!

Bobby's is a popular frozen-custard stand in a nearby town. We had become known for our love of Bobby's because we often posted pictures of ourselves when we were there. At his retirement party Butch received many gift cards for Bobby's. Tyler brought this treat packed in ice so it wouldn't melt. It took quite an effort to pull this off. I was very thankful but couldn't eat much. By now, my stomach was getting used to having nothing in it.

Update: July 12: This is the song for the day/week/ life. Please listen. If you've never heard this song, it's time you did. This is me—every single day. The song is "Oceans (Where Feet May Fail)" by Hillsong United. These are the lyrics of the bridge.

Spirit lead me where my trust is without borders.
Let me walk upon the waters
Wherever you would call me
Take me deeper than my feet could ever wander,

And my faith will be made stronger
In the presence of my Savior

Update: 11:26 p.m. We are turning a corner! Today they have lowered the oxygen level on the ventilator to as low as they will go before extubating. The pressure they use to push the oxygen into the lung is almost as low as it will go. They have discontinued everything going into his central line except pain medication, sedation medication, antibiotics, and fluids. They are discussing removing a chest tube or two. The word *wean* has been used several times today. That is a very good word.

My mom is doing a little better. She is very frail but better even than yesterday.

I feel as if a thousand pounds has been lifted from my chest and my heart. I've cried so many tears, had so many adrenaline dumps from scares, avoid food and drink because my body rejects this, and have had a total of about twelve hours of sleep since Monday. But the presence of God is surrounding us in this room. Thank you for praying. Please don't stop. Butch still has a long way to go.

Sunday, July 13

Update: 5:16 a.m. Butch's fever is still climbing. Please pray they find the source and treat it quickly.

Update: 6:13 a.m. Every time 6:00 to 8:00 a.m. rolls around, all visitors must leave the ICU for the shift change/report. During the a.m. time, the waiting room has a smattering of sleeping family members of loved ones. I am thankful for my cubby behind Butch's bed where I can still sleep with him even if it's several feet away.

Butch's fever is pretty high. They don't know the source, so they will most likely do another CT scan this morning. They suspect it's from his lungs. His lungs need to heal. All infection, no matter where in his body—gone. In Jesus's name.

Update: 8:25 a.m. Going down for CT. Looking at lungs, brain, and abdomen. Fever very high. Pray.

Update: 12:56 p.m. CT scan reveals no head or abdominal issues. Praise God! They believe that the fever stems from the lungs, which, believe it or not, is good news. His lungs show slight improvement from Thursday. Now the biggest concern, apart from his lungs healing, is that they will be able to bring him out of sedation enough to test his ability to move his feet, hands, and limbs. He's been on super sedatives for quite a while, and they want to try to keep as much muscle tone as possible. Keep praying!

Update: 6:41 p.m. This is my daughter holding my mother's hand. The picture was taken today. Please pray for my mommy. She is being admitted to ICU. They have found blood in her digestive tract.

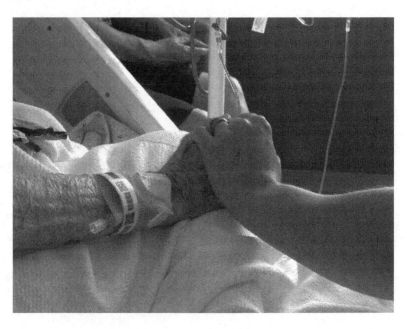

My daughter Tiffany holding my mother's hand.

Update: July 13: Through this storm at Barnes ICU, I am grieving that I can't also be with my very ill, very frail mom in the hospital. God is sending angels of mercy in the form of my daughter Tiffany, cousins Carol, Barb, and Jeri Lou, and many friends who are visiting her, sitting with her, reassuring her, but I know she wants her daughter with her, and I just can't leave. Butch is still not out of the woods. Oh Jesus, I love my mom!

Update: July 13: We have created a Flat Butch fan page on Facebook. Flat Butch refers to the pictures on skewers that were in all of the centerpieces at Butch's retirement party. Even before the accident, Flat Butch was becoming famous. To become part of the phenomenon, search Flat Butch here (on

Facebook) and join the fun. When Butch wakes up,
he's going to love it! By the way, thank you, Janna
and Tyler, for making Flat Butch a reality!

The Flat Butch phenomenon had begun. We created this special
Facebook group to invite people to pray for my husband. What
happened was far more than we ever imagined. Our friend Gena,
who is Tyler's mother-in-law and a friend with whom Butch and I
had worked for years in the school districts, made several Flat Butch
sticks for people to take with them. They were free, and people
were encouraged to take as many as they wanted. Unfortunately,
the chosen distribution site for these Flat Butches was the funeral
home that Tyler and Janna owned. When the announcement was
made that these were available for pickup at the Pitchford Funeral
Home, the response was extreme. People thought Butch had died.
Though he was in extremely critical condition, he was still with us.
We immediately clarified the reason for this distribution site, noting
Gena was working there, answering phones during the day, and that
it was a central location.

Having a good friend who is the owner of a funeral home can
cause a lot of misunderstanding, as we learned. Tyler was also at
the first hospital where Butch was taken immediately after he fell.
People walked into the emergency waiting room, saw Tyler, and
froze, thinking he was there on official business. But Tyler is golden.
He and Janna and her parents, Gena and Tom, are amazing friends
who helped throughout this ordeal in ways I can never repay, as did
many others.

> **Update: 6:57 p.m.** I ate three-quarters of a
> hamburger and almost a whole order of fries from
> the cafeteria.

The response to this one little Facebook post was amazing. I had
no idea how many people were monitoring my eating status. But this

was huge. I existed in a constant state of concern for my husband and my mom, feeling helpless in both situations. I found it terribly difficult to eat, because my stomach was in knots.

Update: 7:25 p.m. Another emotional roller coaster of a day. While my husband is improving, my mom is being admitted to the ICU at Alton Memorial. Apparently it was appalling that she was transported from Barnes to Rosewood. She is very sick but with something that is treatable. My poor mom. But she had Barb, Carol, Nonie, Tiff, Jeremy, Logan, Dennis, and Kelly to help her through the day. Dennis brought his guitar, and they sang for quite a while. Thank you.

After a scary morning, Butch was given a bath, a shave (the nurse spared his mustache), and some more scary medical stuff. Butch is stable and making headway. They have reduced the oxygen even lower than I reported earlier, and he is tolerating the new level well. At one point when Kristi and I were in the room, he opened his eyes a little—only for a moment, but he opened them.

Specific prayer requests: First, that the blood in his lungs will be taken care of by his body before infection settles in. He has no sign of infection yet. Miraculous. Second, that his pain will be controllable so he can breathe and won't experience collapsed lungs again once he's extubated. Third, that when they do extubate, they will be successful and he won't have to be intubated again.

Thank you all so much. Your prayers are moving heaven on Butch's behalf. There is a spiritual battle going on, and we are making headway! God is victorious!

Update: 10:42 p.m. Husband in ICU at Barnes. Mom in ICU at Alton Memorial Hospital. I am sitting in my cubby, feeling peaceful, full of faith and joy.

Those of you who are following this story closely, please understand that this comes only from prayer warriors storming heaven on our behalf. I've spent so many posts this week urgently calling warriors to battle for Butch and Mom. In this calm moment I want to tell all of you that God is real. Don't try to tell me He isn't. I feel Him. I hear Him. I know Him. He is sustaining all of us during this storm. He has touched my husband's body over and over.

I am praying for all of you as well—praying that God will bless your faithfulness in this war, praying that if you are following this story and don't know Jesus as your savior, our experience will draw you to seek Him. I am eager to talk with you if you have questions. Trust me, if Butch knew that one person would trust Jesus because of this accident, he would go through it willingly.

I love you all and can't wait to share the full story of what's happened this week. You really can't make this stuff up.

Monday, July 14

Update: 6:35 a.m. Butch had a relatively quiet night. They did a breathing test around 4:30 a.m. to determine how well he will be able to breathe without the ventilator. He didn't do well. His nurse says they didn't expect him to pass yet, but this will exercise his lungs. Please pray for his lungs to heal.

I am going to try to leave for a bit to visit my mom today. I am so torn. I feel like my heart is being ripped apart. Please pray that I can hold it together when I see her so she doesn't worry more than she already does. I can act, but my mom reads straight through me.

Update: 8:35 a.m. It's been a week. Butch is still sedated and on life support. They have found what they believe to be a very small amount of blood on his brain but don't think it's bleeding anymore. That is a new prayer concern.

Sometimes people can say well-meaning things and inflict pain on a person. Even those who work in the health care field and regularly deal with pain and suffering can be guilty of this. When I arrived in the ICU to see my mom and discovered she was in contact isolation, I was in disbelief. I hadn't been able to see her for several days, and in that time she had been through so much. She was about to be taken down for a procedure, and I couldn't be with her. As I stood at the door of her ICU room, the nurse behind the desk told me I could go in if I donned a gown and gloves. I explained the situation with my husband and said I was concerned about transmitting something to him. She chastised me for being there with my mom when clearly my place was with my husband. Goodness. I hadn't thought of that.

I had purchased a stuffed Hello Kitty doll to give to my mom. She had spent a lot of time in Japan, and while there she had fallen in love with this character. I told her that this was my representative and that she should know I was always thinking of her even though I couldn't be with her very much at this time. I told her that every time she looked at that Hello Kitty, she would know that I loved her. Then, taking the well-meaning advice of that ICU nurse, I headed back to Barnes Hospital to be with my husband.

> **Update: 1:36 p.m.** Just went to see mom. Had to talk from the door of her ICU room due to isolation. First thing I wanted to do when I left? Call Butch. Sigh.

> **Update: 3:20 p.m.** The brain bleed is becoming a concern. They're going to do a neurological exam sometime this evening. Please pray. Hard.

> **Update: 9:37 p.m.** In Jesus's name, please pray that Butch will respond to commands when brought out of sedation. In Jesus's name, I'm calling on prayer warriors yet again to storm heaven.

A new fear was emerging. When the doctors attempted to get a response from Butch by using painful stimuli, they got none. I heard one nurse say in passing, "I hate it when we save their lives but there's nothing in there." I couldn't believe what I had just heard. Surely, after all we had been through, God wouldn't allow Butch to be brain dead, would He? I asked questions of every person who entered his room. The ICU doctor, a different one now because they rotated every week, said he was concerned that Butch wasn't responding. The trauma doctor said, "Of course he's not responding.

He's sedated." The neurologist said the same thing. I didn't know who to believe.

I was on yet another roller coaster, and I wanted to get off. I'd had several adrenaline dumps in the past week, and my body couldn't take any more. Each time I heard the slightest negative report, my body would have that fight-or-flight response, causing my stomach to churn and my heart to race. My head would spin and my ears would ring. My health was being affected, but I had no time to address this problem. I had to make several decisions daily about Butch's care, signing consent forms for this and that. At many points I also had to give consent over the phone for my mom's care. Finally, I officially turned over the decision-making power to my cousin Carol. She became the first contact for my mom's care until things settled down with my husband. If something happened with my mom, the hospital would call Carol, and she would call me. I hated this arrangement, but it was the only thing I could do.

CHAPTER 6

It was time to settle in for the evening, but there was a lot of commotion in the room next door to Butch. When patients were fairly stable, one nurse was assigned to two of them at a time. However, when one of the patients was in trouble, the original nurse took that patient, and another nurse covered the stabler patient. Up to this point, Butch had often been the unstable patient requiring one nurse's undivided attention. This evening, his next-door neighbor was that person. I could tell things weren't going well for this young man. It was very upsetting to hear and to see. I kissed Butch's forehead, lay down on the couch in my little cubby, and prayed for Butch, my mom, and this young man.

Tuesday, July 15

> **Update: 4:30 a.m.** A mother lost a child today. In the room next to us, a young man lost his life to a horrendous motorcycle accident. When the mother let out an all-too-familiar wail, I knew. There is only one thing that elicits that deep, soul-wrenching, heartbreaking cry. Please pray for this family. I don't know them. Jesus does.

I often saw death in this place. Too many times it was a young person who lost his or her life. Sometimes I was that stranger in the waiting room, wondering what was going on with a family's loved one, like those watching us in the original emergency waiting room at the first hospital. As I sat in this ICU waiting room, I observed. A culture and a rhythm emerged. Everyone had his or her own story, but we were the same. While sitting and watching, I wrote about this phenomenon. Writing is a way for me to cope with extreme emotion. It is cathartic. As I sat in a recliner, wrapped in a hospital blanket, taking everything in, afraid to feel, I wrote. I called this little essay "ICU Waiting Room Culture."

There is a definite order to things in this place where time is irrelevant and people are desperate. Families come and go for different reasons. Sometimes a loved one is in the ICU for a short time and is transferred to a regular room. Those are the happiest cases. I rejoice for the woman whose husband got to leave yesterday to go to a different floor. Then there is the most devastating reason families leave the ICU waiting room. I cry with them every time—privately.

Even though time is irrelevant here, we are ruled by the clock. Between 6:00 and 8:00 a.m. and p.m. all visitors must leave the ICU and go to the waiting room. This is when people stake out spots for themselves and their families for the day. I try to find a spot that is private and has an electrical outlet. If it has a couch or a recliner, that's perfect. If not, the regular chairs can be manipulated to be fairly comfortable, even for a short nap during the day.

Around 7:30 a.m., hospital personnel move everyone up to the front of the waiting room so housekeeping can clean. Thankfully, our previously claimed spots are protected if we leave stuff in them. Workers clean around our things. After cleaning is done, we all return to our little private areas, resuming what we do to pass the time. I pray, post on Facebook, visit with those who come by, and maybe nap a little.

As soon as 8:00 a.m. comes, I go right back to Butch's room. The doctors come by for their morning rounds between ten and twelve. That's when the day's emotion is determined. Will there be tests? Do they see improvement? Do they not see improvement? Why is this happening? Why is this not happening? What are they going to do to make everything okay? Oh doctors, I know you have a huge amount of education and some of you have a ton of experience. But I know the Great Physician who holds my husband in His hands. He makes the decisions. He determines the pace of healing. He has this. He is guiding your minds and your hands in treating my husband. I am so very thankful for all of you. But I am so much more thankful for my heavenly Father, who loves us all more than we could possibly imagine.

After rounds, depending on what we learn, our day moves on with tests, visits to our loved ones, visits with family and friends, constantly in and out of the patients' rooms. We talk to the nurse for reassurance, try to eat something, try to drink something, and talk to the nurse again. "What are you doing? How is he doing?" Time marches on. But time is irrelevant.

The 6:00-to-8:00-p.m. shift comes, and once again we must leave the ICU and go to the waiting room. This time, finding a spot is more difficult. Those who do not stay all night in the rooms with their loved ones must find spots in the waiting room to sleep. If they find a spot with a couch or a recliner, they have a small chance of getting some rest—that is, if their loved ones are stable and able to rest as well.

Every day there is a group of people who are visibly more upset. They feel concern and worry. They have heard bad news, the worst news, and when that happens, all in the room identify with that family. We privately or publicly pray for/with them. While doing that, we hold on to hope and have faith that we won't be that family. Ever.

Update: 7:02 a.m. From *Jesus Calling*: "Do not worry about tomorrow! This is not a suggestion but a command. I divided time into days and nights so that you would have manageable portions of life to handle. My grace is sufficient for you, but its sufficiency is for only one day at a time. When you worry about the future, you heap day upon day of troubles onto your flimsy frame. You stagger under this heavy load, which I never intended you to carry. Throw off this oppressive burden with one quick thrust of trust. Anxious thoughts meander about and crisscross in your brain, but trusting Me brings you directly into My Presence. As you thus affirm your faith, shackles of worry fall off instantly. Enjoy My Presence continually by trusting Me at all times" (Young, p. 206).

I plan to read this continually today. I think it may be possible that when this was written, God knew that this was exactly what this worried/concerned/scared wife needed to hear while sitting in the ICU waiting room today. Isn't He the most amazing heavenly Father?

Update: 8:31 a.m. In around an hour they will take Butch down for a CT to check out the brain bleed. I have faith that it will be of no importance. In Jesus's name.

Update: 10:38 a.m. Prayer warriors, unite. All sedation is off to see if he will wake up. Please pray for him to wake up.

Update: 1:51 p.m. The best update ever! Prayer warriors, you rock. God rocks! The brain bleed is smaller. Butch is waking up and responding. He moved his fingers on command! He focused on my face! He smiled at me several times. Thank you. The next step is to get him off of the breathing tube. A million pounds is off my chest right now. It's not over by far. Please keep praying. But this is the first time since Monday, July 7, that I've breathed easy. Praise God!

Also, thank you so much, Pastor Roy and the Abundant Life staff, for blessing me not only with your visit but also with my first-ever Crown Candy BLT. Thank you.

That BLT sandwich contained a pound of bacon. It's Crown Candy's signature sandwich. I could eat only a few bites, but I shared it with my daughter-in-law Kelli, who had made it her job to be with me at the hospital all day, every day, so I wouldn't be alone. Her mom took care of our granddaughters, Elle and Paisley, so Kelli could be with me. Kelli worked for her church as the children's ministry coordinator, so much of her job could be done from her laptop in the ICU waiting room. Joe worked for Washington University just down the street, so he could hop on the Metro-link train and be at the hospital in five minutes. He also spent a lot of time working from his laptop in the waiting room. The other kids and their spouses weren't as blessed with jobs that allowed them to work anywhere from their laptops, so they weren't able to be at the hospital during the day as much but tried to be there in the evenings.

We had settled into a routine of sorts by this time. It had been a week and a day since the accident. At this point Butch was improving. He was still unconscious and on life support but was stable. My mom was stable in the hospital across the river. My daughter Tiffany, my cousins Carol, Barb, and Jeri Lou, along with my friends Kelly and Dennis, spent a lot of time with my mom so I could stay with Butch.

> **Update: 10:50 p.m.** Today is the day my husband came back to me, even in a groggy state. For a little while, he looked right into my eyes, smiled at me, and tried to squeeze my hand. I kissed his lips, and he tried to kiss back. Today, July 15, my husband came back to me. God is so very good.

> Butch is still sedated but not as deeply. They do this to keep him comfortable because of the level of pain he will experience when he is fully awake. He is tough, but he needs to breathe through the pain to keep his lungs inflated. We don't want another collapsed lung. Nor do we want pneumonia.

During this time, we will limit the number of visitors to Butch's room. We love to see you, but overstimulation is not a good thing. If you come to the hospital, please come to the waiting room. Text me if I'm not there. I will be in his room, the waiting room, or the bathroom.

I believe I will sleep more peacefully tonight. Tomorrow they may extubate. Tomorrow will be a big day. Please continue to pray because he still has a long road ahead of him.

One more thing: I pray for all of you who are following this story. If you don't have a relationship with God, you need to. We all need Him. If this hasn't convinced you, what on earth will?

One more thing before I sign off and go to sleep: There is a young man here named Adam. His family shared his story with me and gave me permission to share it with you. Two weeks ago his truck fell on him. He has been here, fighting for his life since then. His body is showing signs of improvement, but his brain is not waking up. Please pray for a complete restoration. This is a Christian family. We visited in the ICU waiting room. They have faith.

Wednesday, July 16

Update: 8:14 a.m. Butch had an uneventful night. He is resting quietly. I slept more last night than probably the first five nights here combined. I don't know what is in store for today—maybe just coasting, maybe extubating. Please continue to pray for my amazing husband and best friend. I'm ready for him to come fully awake, to lose the life support, and to talk to me. I miss him.

Update: 11:29 a.m. Butch is still quiet and stable. They are going to put him in a special chair today—even sedated. This will help him to breathe and hopefully to wake up a little better. The biggest prayer concern is now for his lungs and his ribs to heal enough for him to be able to breathe on his own. This is another concern: there is talk about moving the ventilator to a tracheotomy instead of down his throat. Given the extent of his injuries, it is taking a little longer for him to be comfortable enough to breathe. This is the reason they had to sedate him a little more: the pain level gets bad, so he becomes agitated. My poor, sweet Butch.

At this point, I am so very thankful. He will heal. He will be 100 percent. I will have him back fully. During this time, I will trust God. He certainly hasn't failed us yet!

Update: 5:00 p.m. Butch is in a special chair for those in his state. They did another breathing trial, which he did not pass. He just has to have more time to heal. The breathing trials exercise his lungs, so they're still good. If things don't change within the next twenty-four hours, he will probably have to have a tracheotomy. This is not bad news. It just means that he needs more time. His injuries are so bad. The sedation is for pain control only. He will make a full recovery, I'm told, but again, it will be a long road by medical standards. But I know God. I suspect Butch will be up and around in no time.

Update: 11:00 p.m. I'm praying for a certain family whose son was badly injured. The past two weeks have been filled with tragedy in the lives of people I know. One family lost two kids in one week. Another lost an only son. Now this. Dear Jesus, please put your arms around everyone involved in all of these situations. Show them your intimate love. Help them through this.

I was painfully aware that my family and I were not the only ones who had suffered or were suffering through difficult times. It seems that when it rains it pours. During this difficult, scary time of my life, so many others were suffering even worse things. I prayed and wept for them as they had done for me. This is what we did for each other. And it helped—a lot.

Update: 11:00 p.m. Butch is still resting and on the ventilator. We started physical therapy today to help with flexibility so that when he is out of sedation he will have less difficulty. I am overwhelmed by the generosity of so many. I won't name them right now. It would take way too long. All I can say is thank you. You have blessed us more than you could possibly know.

My prayer request for Butch is that he will heal soon. In Jesus's name. Also, please pray for Eddie. I met his family today.

By this time, I had received boxes and baskets full of wonderful surprises. People sent care packages filled with love, trying to make my stay with Butch a little more comfortable. I got all kinds of food, reading material, Chapsticks, wet wipes, gum, hand sanitizers—you name it. The hospital had a shower that family members of patients could reserve and even provided towels. Each time I used the shower I would notice how much my body was shrinking. Under normal circumstances I would be happy about this because like most women, I'm always trying to lose weight. However, this was definitely not the way to accomplish weight loss. I was weak. Several times during those long, hot showers I almost passed out. That would not have been good because it would have been a long time before anyone checked on me.

By now, we had met a nurse who became our favorite. Gayla took patient care to a level I had never experienced. The first thing she did with Butch was to create a hilarious-looking sling for his arms. The device looked like socks hanging from IV poles. She hoisted his arms into the sling to fight the swelling. His hands were swollen, and his fingers looked like sausages. We called him Touchdown Butch because while in this contraption, he looked like he was signaling a touchdown. He was unaware of this, but we all knew that if he were awake enough, he would have appreciated our sense of humor.

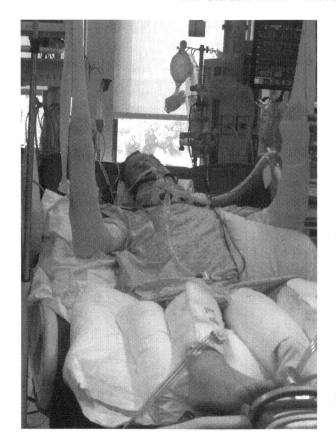

Touchdown Butch

Update: 11:48 p.m. I'm feeling uneasy tonight. With miracle after miracle, I know he is in God's hands. I'm lying right behind him in my cubby, missing him desperately. Maybe it's being tired. Maybe it's the constant roller coaster with adrenaline dump after adrenaline dump that's had nowhere to go because it happens so often. Maybe it's because I want him awake and breathing on his own now. We've seen such upward strides. Why do I feel so uneasy?

We had enjoyed a few quiet days, but I couldn't shake the feeling that something was off. Mom was stable; Butch was stable. What was it? I didn't know this, but yet another storm, bigger than the last, was brewing. It didn't hit for a bit, but it was definitely coming—silently, undetected, and powerful.

CHAPTER

Thursday, July 17

Update: 1:05 a.m. I think I understand my uneasiness now. Butch just had a coughing fit. It was scary. Until Butch's accident, I didn't know people coughed on a vent. His torso rose off the bed. His face turned bright red. He looked at me as if to say, "Do something." They suctioned him and it helped. What I didn't know is that they had completely stopped one of his pain meds today, and he tolerated that pretty well—until this coughing episode. He bit down on the tube. At least he released when they asked. He'd bite. They'd say, "Open your mouth, Butch," and he'd open his mouth. He'd bite and so on. What was most troubling was that I caught a glimpse of the level of pain he suffers when he is on only light sedation and fewer pain meds. His face contorts with pain. His breathing is affected even on the ventilator. Once again, I'm calling all warriors to storm heaven. Pain keeps him from breathing deeply. Pneumonia is a threat. In Jesus's name, please heal him. Please take away this unbelievable pain. In Jesus's name.

Update: 6:22 a.m. Good morning. After Butch had his bump in the road last night, they gave him quite a bit of pain medication and a little more sedation. They have always known that the difficulty will be controlling his pain. They had talked about an epidural, which is very effective for pain control, but he has a fractured T6 vertebra. They've pretty much ruled out an epidural, and honestly I'm a little relieved. I've had reservations about that from the first day, and I said that to my family.

When I was standing by his bed during his rough patch last night, he kept moving his head toward me, looking at me. I don't know if it's good that he's trying to get to me or if it's bad because it causes him to be a little agitated.

Today his central line is showing more signs of infection. They are watching it closely but may decide to remove it. They've also sent more "stuff" down for cultures to determine if he has pneumonia. This is a common occurrence. In Jesus's name.

Thank you all so much for encouraging words and for praying. Last night after this episode, my spirit calmed down. It is impossible to know how far the support for Butch and our family extends. I am humbled and thankful.

Update: 8:49 a.m. It looks like Mom will go to a new facility for rehab. Doctor Green is being very supportive and says he thinks she should make good strides toward getting stronger. I love Doctor Green—and all of you for praying for her.

octor Green had been my mom's doctor for years. He treated her as if she were his mother. He gave me hope. His goal was to get her well enough to move back into her apartment. However, there was no apartment now. I had not told my mom this, because I believed she would give up if she knew. Mom loved her apartment and kept asking if everything was okay there. We lied to her regularly, assuring her everything was fine. In fact, all of her belongings had been hastily moved to the basement of Kristi's house. I planned to reapply for an apartment in the same facility if and when my mom showed enough improvement that she could move back into such a place. I knew it would be weeks before that happened, so we planned to coast, withholding the truth as long as necessary. I hated lying to my mom, but we all agreed that this was best for her. For now, we would see what happened when she was transferred to a different rehab facility.

The ICU attending physician had come to talk to me about the long-term plan for Butch. Fortunately, Tiffany was with me during this conversation and put a positive spin on what was said. We were told that because of the amount of time Butch has been and would continue to be in bed, he would continue to get weaker and to lose muscle tone. His body was already showing signs of this deconditioning syndrome. His muscular legs were shrinking, and his feet were swelling. He hadn't moved much at all since the accident. Because he was unconscious, we had to move his joints for him, but this was difficult. I had been taught how to do this, but with all of the tubes in Butch, I was hesitant. I didn't know if I was causing him more pain. I did my job, but this was not the same as weight-bearing exercise. So the message was that, after he was well enough, he would have to go to a rehabilitation facility to get stronger and to begin walking and feeding himself again. If everything went well, the doctor said, Butch might be home by the end of October. This was July. Wow.

After the doctor left, Tiffany reminded me that school would be starting toward the end of August. She pointed out that it would be easier for me to return to work if Butch was getting care in a rehab facility and growing stronger so that when he came home he would be much more independent. I hadn't thought about this plan, but it made sense. I just wanted my husband home and my life back to normal. October seemed so far away.

Butch had been coughing a lot. He was coughing up a ton of yucky stuff, which concerned everyone. It was so strange to watch a person on a ventilator cough like that. He had to be suctioned often, which wasn't pleasant for him. A nurse, a doctor, or a respiratory therapist would push a tube down his throat through the ventilator tube into his lungs and then suction. It was torture.

> **Update: 12:34 p.m.** I just talked to the doctor. They are going to do a bronchoscope and take out a mucous sample from Butch's lung to see what kind of stuff is growing in there. Then a little later they will do a tracheotomy. This doesn't bother me so much. It's obvious that he will not be able to do without the ventilator anytime soon, so this is the best, safest, less irritating option. His injuries won't let him breathe. The most troubling thing I heard today was that without God's intervention, it will be several months at least before he comes home. He will spend quite a bit of time in rehab, being weaned off the ventilator. I serve a mighty God who is the Great Physician. He can have Butch home whenever His timing allows it. My timing is before the end of August. In Jesus's name.

> **Update: 3:18 p.m.** Prayer warriors, please join me in storming heaven. They've decided to wait a few days to do the tracheotomy to give Butch a chance. We have a window, and now we need a miracle. What a testimony to the doctors and the nurses

if they could avoid this procedure because he has improved so much!

Update: 11:29 p.m. A fairly quiet day. Butch still struggles to breathe. Part of the problem I believe, is that he is doing what the doctor calls "bucking the vent." Who wants that thing down their throat?

I came in around 10:00 p.m. from the waiting room after visiting with a lady whose mom is in the room next to Butch. We talked a ton and discovered we have quite a bit in common. She has a lot going on right now like I do. I think we knew just by looking at each other and started talking. When I came to Butch's room, they were giving him a bath. (Kelli, the curtains were closed, and there were a few sets of feet. You know what I mean.) My heart jumps when that happens. Giving Butch a bath is an ordeal. He has to be log-rolled, and it's painful and frightening for him. He hurts, and when they put the bed down flat he struggles to breathe.

Then something wonderful happened. He opened his eyes. When he saw me, we held eye contact for several minutes while they were working with him. It was obvious that he was in a lot of pain. He just held our gaze. I carefully caressed his face and his shoulders. I lightly placed my hand on his chest and told him he was going to be okay. I told him that we know he is in pain and that they are trying to make it stop hurting. He understood me.

The nurse gave him more pain medication, and he drifted, holding our gaze until mercifully he finally went to sleep.

I needed that so very badly. I miss him so much. Please keep praying for his pain and his breathing. He definitely does have pneumonia. They are giving him antibiotics, starting tonight.

Good night. I believe it will be a quiet night.

Friday, July 18

Update: 6:15 a.m. My last post was at 11:29 p.m. last night. Until 5:58 this morning, I slept uninterrupted. Thank you all for praying for me to have rest. Prayer works.

On my way out to the waiting room (no visitors in ICU from 6:00 to 8:00 a.m.), I talked to Butch's nurse. She said he had another breathing trial last night and did "really good." She didn't define that, but it has to be better than "failed," right?

I cling to the little baby steps—those steps that move him forward and upward. This is a marathon. God's timing is perfect. Having that moment with Butch last night when we gazed into each other's eyes, communicating at a depth that only husband and wife can, was my medicine.

Surgery today on his left wrist and possibly his right. Do you know what's awesome? That he is stable enough that they can go in and fix something as non-life-threatening as a wrist! Praise God!

Update: 9:19 a.m. Prayer warriors, it's working! Butch passed his breathing test, and today they are controlling his pain with very minimal sedation and oral pain medication (given through a tube to his stomach). I can't stress enough how much of a leap this is even from yesterday. If they can control his pain and he can keep passing his breathing tests, the long-term hospital stay may be shortened. Thank you—again. God's timing is perfect, and He is always good, no matter what. Even when things don't go the way we want, God is always good.

This is my message to all who will hear it. No matter what happens, even when the worst things take place in our lives, God is always good. We were feeling pretty positive at this point. Butch had shown signs that his mind was intact, and his lungs seemed to be improving. My mom was improving enough to be moved to a rehab facility. Instead of being in ICU, my husband and my mom might be in rehab facilities. Rehabilitation facilities are not all the same. The type appropriate for my mom was not even close to what my husband would need. My mom would be in Illinois, and my husband would be in Missouri. I would be traveling back and forth between the two. But this would mean progress, and I was okay with that.

My mom had made slow but steady improvement. My cousin had given her a makeover because my younger brother was coming from Florida for a visit. He had gone through a painful divorce a few years earlier and now had a wonderful girlfriend whom he wanted the family to meet. Because Mom had been in the hospital for two months, her hair needed attention. She wanted to look her best for her daughter-in-law-to-be, which I interpreted as an extremely good sign. This had to mean she felt at least a little better.

> **Update: 9:25 a.m.** Lots of good news about Mom today. I went to see her yesterday. When I walked into her room at the hospital, she was sitting in a chair, getting a haircut from my cousin. Last Friday, I witnessed her inability to roll over in her hospital bed. Today she should be moved to the new facility for rehab. Doctor G's goal is to get her back home. Again, God is good. Even if things don't work out like we want, He is good.

> Just a sidenote: Flat Butch is becoming part of the shift-change report. Whenever he gets a new nurse, she already knows about him because they talk about him in the report!

> **Update: 1:47 p.m.** They just took Butch down for surgery on his left wrist and possibly his right. It was hard to watch them take him. The surgery will take four to six hours. Please pray for complete healing.

> They tried another breathing test. He lasted twenty minutes and got really tired. This was a different type of test—more challenging. They are going to give him two more days, but without God intervening, he will have to have a tracheotomy. This will not slow his recovery. Actually, if he has to stay on a ventilator for a while longer, this is a much better option. I'm at peace with this decision only if God doesn't intervene. His timing is perfect, and I totally trust the sovereign God I serve!

We've had some more moments of eye contact. Kelli came back, and he diverted his eyes from mine to hers. His heart rate slowed when he looked at her. My story is that looking into my eyes makes his heart race, and I'm sticking to it.

Update: 6:20 p.m. Butch is out of surgery. It took about five hours. His right wrist/hand has pins, plates, and screws, and the surgeon said he should have full use. I told her that this is his throttle hand for the motorcycle, and she groaned, saying she sees a lot of nasty stuff due to motorcycles.

His left was fine with just a cast. Now we need to focus on healing/pain control/breathing. They are going to wait until Sunday to do the tracheotomy, giving him every possible chance to come off the ventilator. If God wants this to happen, it will happen. If not, I'm okay with that.

Today the social worker visited with me about choosing a rehab hospital. Please pray for guidance.

Update: 11:02 p.m. After looking at rehab hospital options, I came in to Butch's room tonight and his nurse said they have high hopes that he will be off the vent without needing a trach! If that happens, we most likely can avoid a rehab hospital altogether. Off the vent means everything is better—and sooner. Once again, I'm asking all prayer warriors to go to battle. What a miracle this would be, glorifying our heavenly Father! We have a small window of opportunity here, so pray!

The goals are that he can breathe on his own, determined by breathing trials, and that he wakes up enough to be able to protect his airway. Though he has been waking up, it's not enough. Now that his surgery is done, they've turned off the sedation completely and are controlling his pain with regular pain medication. The next couple of days are crucial. In Jesus's name!

Update: 11:41 p.m. Flat Butch has become quite a phenomenon. In case you don't know, it grew out of shenanigans involving the pictures from his retirement party. They were pictures from his school career, placed on skewers poking out of the centerpieces on the tables. People had fun with them. Before Butch's accident, the pictures were already making their way all over the St. Louis metropolitan area on the cake hunt with the Pitchford family. When the accident happened, the craze took off. There is now a Facebook group called Flat Butch. This is based on the children's book *Flat Stanley*. These pictures of Butch are either paper on sticks or images on cell phones, and he is all over the country. If you don't belong to Flat Butch on Facebook, please consider joining. The site is open to everyone. Just search it and request to join. Then take Flat Butch with you to different places and take a picture or two with him. Be creative! #flatbutch #mustacheofpower

My husband's picture had been captured with people all over the country and the rest of the world. This had become such a phenomenon that the local newspaper picked up the story and did a spread on the front page. This was a fun thing for people to do, and it also built awareness for prayer. Doctors and nurses were telling us that we had seen miraculous events take place. God was clearly intervening, and the thousands of prayer warriors storming heaven on Butch's behalf were the reason. The improvement we saw in Butch and in my mom created a brief reprieve for me—a time to regroup, to gather strength, and to build up my faith. That silent storm was still brewing, gaining power. I would need the renewed strength and faith for what was to come.

CHAPTER 8

Saturday, July 19

Update: 6:15 a.m. Butch didn't pass his breathing test this morning. He also didn't wake up enough. They had to sedate him to put in a new central line, and he was on pain medication and medication to help him sleep. I guess it's reasonable that waking up wouldn't be too easy for him at this point. Plus he had surgery yesterday afternoon. Please help me and keep praying that he will wake up enough and will breathe within the parameters they want so he can get that tube out of his throat.

Update: 2:26 p.m. Taking up residence in a teaching hospital can be awesome and scary. I shared with you the devotion from *Jesus Calling* on Tuesday. It was specific for me in my situation on that day. It seemed so, anyway. Three days have passed. I'd like to say that I've had no fear, no panic, no worry, no sorrow since that clear message from God, but I'd be less than honest. I hear scary things. I have to make scary decisions. I see scary things happen to my husband. It's scary. Oh, but God! This is today's devotion from *Jesus Calling*. I don't use this as a replacement for the Bible, but it is really good.

"Bring me all your feelings, even the ones you wish you didn't have. Fear and anxiety still plague you. Feelings per se are not sinful, but they can be temptations to sin. Blazing missiles of fear fly at you day and night. [You better believe it.] These attacks from the evil one come at you relentlessly. [Yes they do.] Use your shield of faith to extinguish these flaming arrows. Affirm your trust in Me, regardless of how you feel. If you persist, your feelings will eventually fall in line with your faith. Do not hide from your fear or pretend it isn't there. Anxiety that you hide in the recesses of your heart will give birth to fear of fear: a monstrous stepchild. Bring your anxieties out into the Light of My Presence, where we can deal with them together. Concentrate on trusting Me, and fearfulness will gradually lose its foothold within you" (Young, p. 210).

Update: 2:30 p.m. Has it really been thirteen days? I've seen families come and families go, some for happy reasons and some for tragic reasons. Three of us families have been here about the same length of time. I've met some incredible people, people who love God and people who need to.

Butch is coasting. They are supporting him while he heals. The miracle here is that the only thing they have to worry about at this point is his lungs. I know that sounds strange, but it could be so much worse. The extent of his injuries and the fact that all ribs, left and right, are fractured have presented a situation where, without a miracle, he will need to have a tracheotomy. I'm okay with that. It's not a setback. Quite the contrary. He will not need to be sedated nearly as much and will be much more comfortable. I want him less sedated. I need him to interact with me as soon as he can. I miss him.

Update: 6:41 p.m. They have determined that Butch has ARDS, or acute respiratory distress syndrome. This can be very serious. They say that they see it often in the unit, but I don't like it. Please continue to pray.

Please pray for Michael. I just met his wife. We have passed each other for two weeks, both of us acknowledging each other's worry with weak nods. She just told me that Michael is not doing well and is not expected to make it. I asked if I could mobilize our prayer warriors. She said yes.

Update: 8:00 p.m. At eight tonight I went back to Butch's room to find a giddy nurse and a wide-eyed Butch. He wiggled both feet, squeezed my hand with his left hand, blinked once for yes and twice for no. His whole face tried to smile when he saw me. Gayla said, "I waited a bit for his pain meds because I knew you needed to see this." Then she hugged me while I cried. She also assured me that ARDS is something they see all the time and that he will be okay. God, please give Gayla an extra special blessing tonight.

Sunday, July 20

Update: 6:30 a.m. A very uneventful night. Butch wakes up each time the nurse talks to him. Because of my interaction with him last night, I was able to sleep several hours. Not sure how many, but I think I need more.

Update: 8:41 a.m. Awake! His eyes are open at least partly most of the time. He is answering questions with blinks—one for yes and two for no. He kept trying to talk to me around the tube. Tomorrow they will still do the tracheotomy even though he passed his breathing trial with flying colors this morning. I am more than okay with this. I am comfortable with it being the safest path. They can wean him off anytime. He was shocked when the nurse told him what day it is. I don't know yet how much he remembers between naps, so I keep encouraging him that he is going to be okay but that he may still hurt some. Duh.

Thank you all for your continued prayers. This is why we are in the place we are in today. I cannot wait to tell him about Flat Butch!

Again I want to say that I love having visitors— but in the waiting room for now. We are strictly limiting who comes back to see him right now so we don't overstimulate him. He is very weak and in a lot of pain.

Update: 9:43 a.m. A miracle has occurred! I am sitting in my cubby crying as I write this. They just did rounds outside Butch's room. I am always invited. The extreme improvement he has made in the last twelve hours has caused them to reconsider the trach. His lungs look good, he passed his breathing trial, and he is completely neurologically responsive. They want to give him every chance to come off the vent without a tracheotomy. It hasn't happened yet, but they are going to postpone and give him a chance. I am in awe of our all-powerful, all-loving Great Physician. Thank you, Lord.

Update: 10:25 a.m. "As the deer pants for the streams of water, so my soul pants for you, O God. My soul thirsts for God, for the living God. When can I go and meet with God?" (Psalm 42:1–2). My answer all day.

Update: 1:02 p.m. Pray! They are extubating him right now!

Update: 2:33 p.m. Off the vent! The situation is precarious. He is very weak. Pray he can stay off!

Update: 4:55 p.m. If you come to the hospital, please go to the waiting room and not to Butch's room in the unit. You can text or message me to let me know you are here. And please pray he can remain off the vent!

Update: 6:00 p.m. I am in awe and wonder of our marvelous God. My husband is off the ventilator, breathing on his own. He is trying to talk, and after about an hour, we were actually able to understand him. The first thing he said to me: "How are you?" That is Butch McGill. His first concern was me.

He is very weak right now, and it's about 50/50 whether he will be able to stay off the vent, according to the nurse. But I know we serve an awesome God, the Great Physician. Miracle after miracle, the evidence of His hand on Butch is real. I am humbled, blown away, astounded, excited. My husband is back. Still a long road ahead, but because of prayer and the hand of God, I have faith that the road won't be that long.

Update: 11:30 p.m. A bump. Butch had an anxiety attack. They have had to put on a BiPAP mask, which forces oxygen down into his lungs. Next step will be intubation if needed. He is calmed down now, so please pray he doesn't need it. In Jesus's name.

Monday, July 21

Update: 6:24 a.m. I am thankful for an excellent nurse. In addition to an anxiety attack, Butch's fever spiked pretty high. It wouldn't show on the oral thermometer, so Gayla insisted on a catheter with a probe for core temp. His fever was high. It was a rocky start to a night filled with balancing O2 levels, heart rate, blood pressure, anxiety. The goal is to keep him off the vent safely. They explained that his condition was like being held underwater. His lungs had a lot of fluid in them, which they took care of with Lasix. While all this was going on, in comes our Doctor T, the one who swooped in that horrible Thursday morning almost two weeks ago. Again, she takes control. With God first, Gayla second, and Doctor Tiffany third, I am happy to report that Butch is still off the vent. Today is key to this being permanent. Thank you for praying!

Update: 6:36 a.m. Yet another family is in the process of losing a loved one up here. I don't know any particulars. Please join me in praying. It's part of the rhythm of this place.

Update: 8:24 a.m. The mandatory 6:00 to 8:00 a.m. exodus of visitors in the ICU is both helpful and stressful—helpful in that it forces all of us back here to leave and to take a breather, stressful in that it forces all of us back here to leave, not knowing what is going on for two hours with our loved ones. Joe came by before heading to work. He and I came back as soon as 8:00 a.m. rolled around. We found Butch resting comfortably, still on the BiPAP, but all of his numbers look fantastic. The nurse feels that the culprit for all of this is a spike in his fever, because he would act the same way on the vent when this happens. So manage the fever, manage everything else.

It's amazing to me how it's possible to be absolutely exhausted and yet invigorated at the same time.

By now my sweet mom had been moved to her new rehabilitation facility. I hadn't been able to go there yet. There was way more going on with Butch than my posts might suggest, and it wasn't feasible for me to leave Barnes Hospital to drive the half-hour it would take to reach my mom. Again, cousins and friends filled the void that my absence created. Mom was supposed to try her hardest to comply with the physical therapy prescribed for her. For my sake, she tried, but it was grueling, painful, and torturous for her physically and emotionally. She wasn't very strong, her appetite was nonexistent, and she was giving up. Mom had been experiencing panic attacks, and they were becoming more frequent. I would try to talk to her on the phone, but her breathing difficulties made it hard for her to speak. I asked my cousin for a description of Mom's room, and what I heard didn't make me very happy. The room was depressing. The facility was older, so the rooms were small and outdated. They were clean but dreary. I knew I needed to try to get across the river to see her as soon as possible.

> **Update: 12:43 p.m.** The ventilator has been removed from Butch's room because he no longer needs it!

The nurses gave Butch a bath. When I came back, they were all giddy and excited. I walked into his room, and this is what they did—with his approval. I cried. They cried. They have caught the Flat Butch fever as well! Ladies, you are amazing. Thank you so much for making my heart smile and for creating such a special moment for Butch and me. We will never forget it.

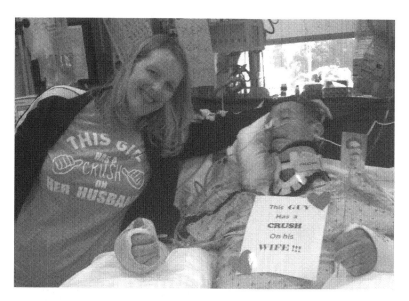

Do you remember the shirt that came in the mail the first week we were in the hospital? I had worn it several times. The nurses had noticed and formed a plan. While I was out of the room for the 6:00 to 8:00 p.m. exodus time, they gave Butch a bath, shaved him, washed his hair, and combed it. Amy, who had gotten me the first couch for my cubby, made a sign and placed it on Butch's chest. When I returned to his room, he was staged and ready for me. He was holding a Flat Butch in his left hand. My shirt said, "This Girl Has a Crush on Her Husband!" The sign said, "This Guy Has a Crush on His Wife!" Medical personnel were lined up outside of his room, watching for my reaction. Several workers were inside the room as well. We had fallen in love with the staff of this ICU, and they had become like family. This was above and beyond what I had ever experienced in any hospital.

> Update: 8:30 p.m. Prayer warriors: Please pray for a young man named Bryce. He has a broken neck and is in surgery right now. He needs the Great Physician to touch him so he willand have no permanent damage. In Jesus's name.

> **Update: 11:29 p.m.** Exactly two weeks ago I was sitting in the waiting room of the trauma, surgical, and burn ICU at Barnes Hospital. I was in shock from what had happened, and I had no idea what the next two weeks would hold. Today has been beyond amazing. I would like to write more, but I keep dozing off. I will try to do better tomorrow, but I can't seem to drag myself away from Butch's bedside unless it's mandated by the ICU staff. Good night.

Tuesday, July 22

Update: 6:42 a.m. Do you know what happens when Butch McGill wakes up from being sedated and on life support for two weeks? He wants to make up for lost time all in one night! Our beloved nurse Gayla was a busy lady last night. Butch wants to eat, sit up, get up and walk, watch the news, play the video games in the room (the monitors are pretty colorful), and exercise. I told them, "He will do more than double what you ask of him." Of course he can't do any of these things yet. A little bit of ICU delirium is setting in, which they told me would happen. Days and nights get mixed up; his sleep cycle is all over the place. Wait. There is no cycle. The man has been awake since yesterday morning. And he talks almost nonstop. They are going to attempt to help him with the day/night cycle by rearranging his room. I didn't even know this was possible, but they will orient his bed so he can see out the window. This will allow us to see each other during the night as well. I love this idea.

All of his vital signs are excellent. Gayla even took his oxygen off for about five minutes to do some things, and his oxygen saturation stayed at 96 percent. This is huge. But the biggest miracle after his surviving this is that he doesn't have a ton of pain. Seriously. We keep asking him if he is in pain, and he says no. Only twice has he asked for medication, and that is for his back. We think it's the compression fracture that is bothering him, but the problem could be that he has been in bed for two weeks. His ribs are broken, but they don't hurt.

Only Jesus! If you are reading this and don't know Jesus, here is yet another miracle that He has done. All broken ribs, no pain. Thank you, Jesus.

When the shift changes, everyone wants to come check on Butch. He has won the hearts of everyone in the unit, and that's before he's totally awake and himself.

As I sit in the waiting room writing this, in my view is Michael's wife, who told me her husband is most likely not going to make it. I see Bryce's father, who came in last night terrified because his son has a broken neck and went through hours and hours of surgery. I see Adam's mom with her Bible on her lap, praying for her son to awaken. And there are the new faces, faces of extreme worry and fear. Those faces are what I looked like only three days ago. This is a very difficult place to live. Our story has a happy outcome. Yesterday three people died back there. Today maybe more. I am humbly thankful for my husband.

I didn't mention in this post the most entertaining part of what happened during the night. Gayla told me later about this little incident. Apparently during the night when I was sound asleep, Butch reverted to middle-school-principal mode. He asked Gayla what time it was. When she told him it was three-thirty, he was concerned that they hadn't said the Pledge of Allegiance yet. Gayla assured him that it was 3:30 a.m., not p.m., but he was not convinced. He would not rest until she said the pledge. Since there was no American flag in the room, he decided that the clock would suffice. So, being the super nurse that she was, Gayla finally faced the clock, placed her right hand over her heart, and said the Pledge of Allegiance. Though it was 3:30 a.m., plenty of people—doctors, nurses—were walking by the room at that moment. They would stop, look questioningly into the room, and Gayla would just say, "Nothing to see here. Move along!" We all had a good laugh when she told us this story.

> **Update: 11:10 p.m.** The Flat Butch phenomenon blows me away. I am so humbled. At this point, there are 1,105 members. Thank you so much for this incredibly fun tribute. I showed Butch many of the pictures today. He got a great kick out of it but was also emotional at the support. I explained that Flat Butch is a reminder to pray for him. That is the true purpose. What a fun way to do this. I can't wait to see where this leads.

Wednesday, July 23

> **Update: 6:24 a.m.** Butch had a quiet night. Our nurse, Gayla, is quite a go-getter. She has been very aggressive in taking care of him, unafraid to step up and do things on her own to ensure his comfort and to speed up his recovery. His absolute favorite (not) is frequent suctioning. This involves inserting a tube through his nose, down his throat, and into the bronchial tubes and cleaning things out—almost hourly. With his injuries, this is a lot of "stuff." The result has been improved breathing, improved comfort, and X-ray evidence that his lungs are much clearer. She is trying to arrange to take him outside for a few minutes this morning. This is no easy feat, requiring portable equipment. She wants to do whatever she can to reset his circadian rhythm. I'm beyond impressed with her care of my husband.

I am starting to feel the effects of little sleep, low nutrition (despite everyone's attempt to feed me), and the emotional toll of having a critically ill husband and mom at the same time. If it weren't for amazing family and friends stepping in and helping, I don't know what I would have done. I can't be in two places at once, and each of these people has needed me. Until I can tell you face-to-face, I want to say "Thank you" in this post to those who have helped me survive this unbelievable ordeal. (You know who you are.) Even though it's not over—not by a long shot—the acute phase of this storm may be getting close to passing. We will need to travel a long road, but again, I'm so thankful to have a road at all.

Please pray for my mom. I was able to leave for a couple of hours yesterday evening to visit her at the rehab facility. She is depressed and ready to give up. I guess being in six health institutions in two months is a little much for anyone. I had to sit down with her and the social worker and explain that she has to comply with therapy. She wants to lie in the bed and sleep all day. She is not eating or drinking. My heart breaks for her. I know part of the problem is that I can't be there right now. The doctor thinks she should be able to gain a lot of strength and stamina, but she has to want it.

Thank you all so much for your prayers and support. I can't even begin to tell you how much it means. I will post a little later about our field trip outside if it happens. Pictures to come.

Gayla and Butch outside of Barnes Hospital.

Update: 8:37 a.m. Gayla pulled it off! We went outside. Butch really enjoyed it. The big joke was how hard we've all worked to remove fluid from his lungs, and now we take him outside where he breathed it back in! It sure is humid today.

I am thankful for an amazing medical staff—especially Gayla—who will go way beyond the norm to ensure success for each patient. Of course we feel like we are special, but that's how good these people are. They make everyone feel that way!

Update: 4:48 p.m. Butch has had his own version of boot camp today. It started with a field trip outside. This is not a normal activity for patients in ICU! Gayla is amazing. When we came back to the room, he stayed in the chair for several hours.

After they put him back in bed and he got comfortable, physical therapy came in to sit him on the edge of the bed. He did several leg exercises, which he performed like a champ. He always wants to do more than they ask.

The real miracle here is that he rarely complains of pain. Do you remember the prayer requests regarding pain? We were told that he would be in excruciating pain when he wakes up. It's not happening. Another miracle. Thank you.

Update: 9:48 p.m. What a day. As you know, it started with a field trip outside, followed by a long time sitting up in a chair and looking out the window of our room. I took a two-hour nap during this time. When they put Butch back in bed, gave him a bath, and got him settled, he started to rest. In came P/T to get him to sit on the side of the bed, dangle his feet, and do some leg exercises. He flew through this. He wanted to do more.

Now the plan for tonight is to give him his 10:00 p.m. meds and let him sleep all night. We both need this. How very blessed we are to be in a place where this is possible. We've had two-and-a-half weeks of constant, round-the-clock bedside nursing care for the most part. He has made such progress.

I can't wait to be able to share in person how God has worked throughout this whole journey. His grace and mercy are abundant. He is still the God of miracles!

One more thing—it's a difficult message. They have clamped down on children under the age of twelve being in the ICU waiting room. They are not allowed. The reason is to protect them from things they can be exposed to. Their immune systems are not developed enough. Security came around tonight and told us and everyone else. My granddaughters were there when they told us.

Good night, Facebook friends. Thank you for all of your prayers. And thank you for making Flat Butch such an incredible, crazy, powerful thing.

Thursday, July 24

Update: 6:11 a.m. Butch slept six hours straight last night. I imagine he was pretty exhausted from his busy day yesterday and from being awake for three days. He is getting impatient. He wants to get up, walk, eat—a good sign. It's still difficult to understand him. His vocal cords are weak from being intubated, and his lungs are still healing. He is very weak, but I can see him getting stronger each day.

Today they will get him on a balancing plank and will slowly stand him on his feet while supporting him. He will bear a little weight but only what he can tolerate. Butch is tough.

Another major milestone for today is the plan to move him to the close observation unit (OU). This is a step down from ICU. This is amazingly wonderful news. It makes me a little nervous after the roller coaster we've been on, but I totally trust this ICU staff. They wouldn't move him out if he wasn't ready, would they?

The nurse who had Butch the first three nights and rode through that very difficult Thursday morning (Bad Thursday) was in the unit this morning. She was so amazing throughout that first week—she cried with us—and came back to check on Butch when she was working a different floor. She was amazed at his progress. God is so good.

Update: 8:26 a.m. Respiratory just came in and turned off the oxygen to see how he does. This is huge.

Update: 9:51 a.m. I want to make God famous!

I was full of joy and gratitude. God's presence was so real and tangible for the whole time we had been in the hospital that the desire welled up in me to give God the glory.

Update: 10:08 a.m. Sorry I'm so sporadic today. I just talked to Butch, and he opened his eyes for a few seconds. What did he say? The Cardinals will be in Chicago. I didn't believe him until I checked the schedule. They start a series with the Cubs tomorrow. First things first.

Update: 11:46 a.m. Three hours with no oxygen; oxygen saturation: 97 percent.

Update: 1:49 p.m. Butch to Harry: "Are you coming here tomorrow?" Harry to Butch: "Yes. Do you want me to bring you something?" Butch to Harry: "Yes. Bring me my bike."

Butch was referring to his Harley-Davidson motorcycle. Butch and Harry had been riding together for decades. Harry's wife and I had joined the fun. A few summers earlier we had ridden to Alaska and back on our motorcycles. It was the trip of a lifetime. We saw incredible scenery and wildlife. So now Butch had mentioned the Cardinals' schedule and his motorcycle. We were making progress!

Update: 10:41 p.m. Kind of an uneventful day. Butch was a little more tired than usual today. I guess being awake for three days and "boot camp" yesterday were a little much. He was not only sleepy but lethargic this evening, though he was wide awake and talking. What really got me was when he looked into my eyes and said, "I love you. Forever." Is it okay for him to see me cry?

Some of our closest and dearest friends, Mark and Dena, came up from Arkansas to see Butch. He was very glad to see them but had a hard time not being groggy. Tomorrow.

Each day a sliver of fear or hesitation sneaks in. Even though I know God is in control and has Butch in his hands (how much more proof do we need?), this wife's heart still has concern. Mark and Dena came to see my mom while I was there tonight—just for a bit. After we left her room, we were standing in the parking lot. I expressed some of the fear I was feeling. Mark reminded me that none of this is in my control and to take one day at a time. Hmm, that reminds me of a post I shared from *Jesus Calling* a week ago about just that. Thank you, Lord. And when I got back to Barnes, Butch said, "I love you. Forever." This could not have come at a better time.

We are still in ICU. I don't know when he will be moved to OU. Thank you for your continued prayers. They sustain us.

Friday, July 25

Update: 6:15 a.m. Good morning! Butch and I both had a pretty good night's sleep. He awoke once and was disoriented. The nurse explained where he was, and he came back around pretty quickly. Sixty to 80 percent of patients who are in ICU for a long time develop ICU psychosis, and Butch is one of them. His has a milder form—he just gets confused. I'm told that it can be as bad as a total personality change, yelling at loved ones and cursing. I'm thankful that Butch's is a milder, calmer form. This is brought on by the disruption in sleep cycle, scary sounds, scary people, procedures, needles, tubes, lights. Also, being sedated for two weeks plays a large part. This is a temporary problem. The nurses and doctors see this every day. They don't get upset when they see it. I don't see it every day. I do get upset when I see it. Thankfully I can already see Butch coming out of this, and it makes my heart smile.

I don't know if he remembers asking Harry to bring his motorcycle today, but I'm pretty sure he wouldn't be able to ride it if Harry brought it. Today is a new day. I don't know if we will stay in ICU today or move. Some of the things they were supposed to do yesterday didn't happen—not because of Butch but because this is a huge place and they couldn't make it to him. So today they will probably do a swallow study to see if he can eat and drink. Physical therapy will be doing things with him as well. I will continue to help him exercise his fingers and continue to try to understand him when he talks. His voice is still so weak from the ventilator, but he is quite adept at communicating with his eyebrows.

Update: 7:56 a.m. I know I've posted a ton about Butch's progress and what God has done. There is another storm in my life concurrent with all of this—my mom. She has been in one hospital or another since May 18. I was able to get away to see her for about an hour last night. She told me she wants to go be with Jesus and Jenny. My heart is breaking. I have to make some decisions in the near future, and I would appreciate having you prayer warriors pray for me for wisdom. I don't know how much longer I should push her to try to get better. Mom thinks she is a burden on me with all that is happening. She doesn't understand that if she dies that will be devastating for me. She is tired of being in pain, tired of struggling to breathe, and I understand. Oh Jesus.

Update: 11:26 a.m. They just finished an ultrasound on Butch's legs. They've discovered a couple of clots in one of them. Please pray that they can resolve these quickly and safely. In Jesus's name.

That storm that had been silently brewing was starting to show itself.

CHAPTER 9

Friday, July 25

Update: 5:07 p.m.: We are all concerned about the clots in Butch's leg. The dilemma is that treating them with blood thinners is contraindicated due to his brain injury. His brain injury is small and not an issue at this point. However, blood thinners could change that. The other option is to place a filter through his femoral artery into the vena cava to stop the clots if they break loose. I'm inclined to prefer this course of treatment. We are waiting for neurosurgery and trauma surgery to weigh in.

I know this happens, but my heart dropped when they told me. He's been through so much and is finally making some progress. Please pray that they can safely and completely resolve this. In Jesus's name.

He also did not pass his swallow test today. He is still a little weak, so his swallowing is a little lacking. So we have homework to do. He responds well to my voice, doing what I tell him to do. (I'm sure this will change eventually.) I am putting on my drill sergeant hat and getting him going on his exercises. He has to get his vocal cords working again to be able to eat. When we mention Bobby's, he brightens up considerably. I don't think we will have trouble getting him ready to pass the test on Monday, dangling Bobby's in front of him.

Update: 8:42 p.m. Butch seems to be a little uncomfortable tonight. He is very sleepy but seems agitated. I'm uneasy. I just want him to be better! I know God's timing is perfect.

We are still waiting on neuro to decide the best course of action for the blood clots in Butch's leg. I know there are others in this hospital, but I want action now!

Please, Lord, continue to protect my husband. Thank you for what you've done so far.

All of the beds in the ICU were designed with a pocket under the part of the mattress behind the patient's back. This enabled X-ray films to be easily slid under the patient for the routine nightly chest X-rays. This little pocket made it easy for me to slide my hand under Butch's back and to massage his sore muscles. When I had done this in the past week, he would sigh in approval over how good it felt. This was one thing I could do to help him feel better. However, that Friday evening, Butch responded very differently. This gesture seemed to agitate him. Also, when I told him that I loved him, he looked at me as if he didn't recognize who I was. Something was way off, but the ICU nurse he had this day (and only this day, because I was not pleased with how he treated my husband) kept telling me that the problem was ICU psychosis and that I shouldn't worry. But Butch's fever was climbing, and he was obviously in pain.

Our friends Mark and Dena were in the room, and they noticed a significant change in him from the day before. So the problem wasn't in my mind. It was real. Finally, I went to find the nurse and requested that he come to the room (he hadn't been there for quite some time) to check on Butch. He confirmed that Butch's fever was climbing rapidly and that he needed medication for pain. However, he still tried to convince me that things were okay and that the psychosis was to blame for Butch's strange behavior.

Mark and Dena left for the evening but promised to return the next morning before they headed back to Arkansas. Mark is the pastor of a church down there and had to get back to prepare for the Sunday service. I didn't want to post anything public on Facebook regarding my fears, so I sent this message privately to my best friend, Kelly.

> **Update: 9:20 p.m.** I'm having a rough night. I just need to express some fears/concerns. Butch's ICU psychosis is really bad tonight. He is agitated and acts like he is having a bad dream. I don't think he knows who I am. They tell me they see this every day with 100 percent of patients who have been in here as long as Butch, but it is just killing me. I'm concerned there may be something more since he did have a brain bleed. He is wasting away to nothing, and he didn't pass his swallow test today. Will try again on Monday. He has two blood clots in his right leg. After what happened to Mom, I'm just uneasy. Sometimes he doesn't know my name.

The night nurse was a wonderful young lady with whom I had also developed quite a relationship. Her name was Andria, and she had Butch several evenings in a row. She and Gayla were the two nurses we had most often, because we requested them when they were working. They took care of me as much as they took care of

Butch. Several times after I fell asleep, Andria would cover me with an extra blanket to make sure I was warm enough. She was amazing.

Saturday, July 26

Around four-thirty in the morning, Andria woke me up. She said, "Judy, I wanted to wake you up because the lights are going to come on and the room is going to fill up very fast. I think Butch has thrown a blood clot to his lungs, and he is in trouble."

> **Update: 4:26 a.m.** Need prayer warriors now if you are awake. Butch may be throwing a clot to the lung. Please pray. In Jesus's name
>
> **Update: 4:41 a.m.** Most likely will re-intubate. Jesus, please intervene.

There I stood, watching as medical personnel surrounded my husband's bed, trying to save his life again. And once again, there was no time to ask me to leave the room. It had been almost three weeks since the accident. We had been through so much, and the storms just kept coming. I had nothing left. I watched the monitor as Butch's blood pressure and oxygen saturation kept dropping. His heart rate and respirations were elevated, desperately trying to deliver oxygen to his body. He was crashing in front of me, and I was utterly helpless. As I watched, I cried out to God with extreme desperation. Was I going to lose him after all that had happened?

Immediately I felt God's presence in the form of a warm blanket surrounding my body. I had the physical sensation of all fear seeping out of the bottoms of my feet. And then I heard His voice. This was not a feeling or a sensation. It was audible. Then God said to me: "I have him." My body relaxed, and I leaned against the counter immediately behind me and watched as the team continued to work on my husband. I didn't know if God meant that He was going to heal Butch or to take him home to be with Him. But I understood the sovereignty of God very well. I knew that no matter what happened, God was in control. He is always good, no matter what.

> **Update: 5:27 a.m.** They have reintubated Butch. His oxygen saturation and blood pressure dropped, and his heart rate, respirations and fever spiked—all very quickly. They are looking at infection or pulmonary embolism. His heart looks okay. I'm okay with him going back on a ventilator as long as he needs it. In Jesus's name, Lord, please heal my husband. I need him. I know he is in your hands and that you love him even more than I.

Andria's shift was over at 6:00 a.m., and she passed the torch to Gayla. When Gayla spoke to me for the first time that morning, her demeanor was completely different than before. She wasn't the smiling, bubbly person who had cared for Butch in several previous days. Her face was solemn, concerned, and focused.

> **Update: 6:24 a.m.** Butch is stable and back on the ventilator at lower settings so they can increase support if needed. He definitely has a new pneumonia, which they will culture and hit with specific antibiotics, and possibly a pulmonary embolism. The doctor assures me that this is just a "bump" and that we will get through it. I said to him, "Poor guy. He's been through so much." The doctor said, "Soon to be a distant memory. He'll be okay." It is amazing how God works. Once again, I'm standing in Butch's room in the early morning, watching a group of people rush in to intervene during a crisis. Once again, I call out to prayer

warriors for urgent intercession. But this time, as I was watching people push this med and that med, rushing around, preparing to intubate, discussing possible reasons for this crisis, I felt an enveloping peace surround me. It felt like a warm blanket. My heart calmed. My mind stopped racing. Fear lifted. I heard God say to me, "I have him." It was as real as the voices of those people working on Butch. Thank you, Jesus, for the way you rushed in to comfort your child. Thank you for loving me enough to calm my fear. Thank you for loving Butch enough that you "have him." And thank you for letting us have Gayla today.

Update: 10:00 a.m. Butch isn't stable enough to go to CT. Looking more and more like a clot. CT of head at bedside ordered ASAP. If clear, they will hit him with blood thinner. He is in a bit of trouble, so please pray hard.

Update: 12:10 p.m. We are not out of the woods. Butch's clinical picture points to a pulmonary embolism. They have him stable for now, but it takes work to keep him this way. His blood pressure keeps dropping. They have cleared his brain for a heparin drip. I asked if they are absolutely sure, and they said yes. They have checked for heart failure—no results yet. They are now taking him down for an emergency CT of his chest, even though he isn't quite stable enough. They are hoping to see a clot that is either accessible to remove or to inject with an anticoagulant, thus taking care of it right there. Thank you for continuing to pray. I will try to keep you all updated as often as I can.

Gayla had little time to talk all day. She worked nonstop to keep Butch alive. I learned later that he was classified as a "full code" all day long. They didn't have to administer CPR physically, but Gayla said they were doing basically the same thing chemically all day long. This explained her demeanor and why she was so focused. She was keeping my husband alive by pushing this medication and that medication all day long. At one point she said to me, "You have to understand we are Barnes Hospital. We are the ones who figure out the most difficult cases. People come to us from all over for this reason. And we can't figure out what is going on with Butch." I thought she was going to cry. I did cry.

> **Update: 4:49 p.m.** We just met with the doctor. There is evidence of small clots passing through the lungs but nothing huge. They are treating with heparin, which is the appropriate course. Butch also has a new infection in his lungs, and as soon as they identify the bacteria, they will treat it appropriately. For now, they are hitting him with broad spectrum antibiotics until they can be more specific. Another concern is sepsis. His symptoms could also be indicative of this, which they will deal with as well.
>
> So for now, we are not out of the woods. However, we are not as deep into the woods as we were twelve hours ago. When God wrapped His arms around me like that warm, calming blanket, I knew that He had Butch in His care. It is still hard for me to go through this, but all of your continuous prayers have certainly sustained us. Thank you. I will keep you posted.
>
> **Update: 10:54 p.m.** What a roller-coaster day. The details would take way too long to relay, but it was

filled with severe fluctuations of blood pressure, heart rate, and respiration rate, temperature spikes, people running in to test this, push that, check his brain, check his heart, get him stable enough to go to CT for his lungs, and on and on. That amazing, supernatural calming blanket that came over me early this morning never left. However, it did not stop me from being emotional. Many tears were shed today—again.

There are several possible explanations for what happened. One is that an infection alone caused this. Another—and there is evidence on the CT scan to support this—is that a clot(s) broke loose, hit his lungs, and dispersed, leaving a trail behind. In addition to the infection in his lungs, Butch also may have the beginning of septicemia. They are treating him as if this were the case, so he is being covered quite well with antibiotics. He seems to be responding already. He is deeply sedated again because he doesn't like the vent. The doctor who intubated him this morning said Butch's right leg works quite well. Evidently he was kicking, not wanting the tube. I can't blame him, but it is keeping him alive. I have a love/hate relationship with that tube.

Right now, I lie in my cubby, once again listening to the rhythm of the ventilator supporting my husband's breathing. I know that this is a bump in the road and that he will soon be off again, breathing on his own—this time permanently. He is stable. We will be in ICU for at least another week, making it a month in here. It's a difficult place to live if you are not sedated, but I am thankful that there is a comfortable place for me to sleep with him in my sight. The nurses and I have become quite close, and they care for me as much as him. Two nurses have told me that they have come in during the middle of the night and covered me with an extra blanket while I sleep. This is quite a place, and I thank God for all of the technology, research, and cutting-edge treatment as well as the amazing personnel who work here. They have saved Butch's life more than once.

One more thing: This is the beginning of today's devotion in *Jesus Calling*: "Relax and let Me lead you through this day. I have everything under control: My control. You tend to peer anxiously into the day that is before you, trying to figure out what to do and when ... When you let *Me* direct your steps, you are set free to enjoy Me and to find what I have prepared for you this day" (Young, p. 217). Well, again the message couldn't be better.

So much had happened in the past three weeks—no, in the past two-and-a-half months. Since my mom fell on May 18, my life had been like a hurricane. Strong winds, powerful waves, and a calm eye of the storm were followed by more strong winds, powerful waves, and another eye of the storm. Most people go through unbelievably rough times. I'm no different. I want to share my story so everyone can see and feel how God intervened, rushing to my rescue when I needed Him most. Some may ask why He didn't keep it all from happening, but how could He show Himself is such powerful ways without the trials and tragedies of our lives?

Let's take inventory. God had revived Butch as he was lying in the yard, possibly breathing life back into him in front of us.

He restored Butch's body, which appeared to have a serious spinal injury. God rescued him from damage to his heart and major vessels when the tension hemopneumothorax pushed everything toward the center of his chest. Though the first ER doctor pushed a chest tube through Butch's lung, it missed his aorta. If his heart and major vessels hadn't been shifted toward the center of his chest, that tube quite possibly could have gone right through the aorta, killing him.

The surgery to remove this badly placed chest tube was minimal, and the doctors didn't have to remove any of Butch's lung. He wasn't extubated in the early morning of Bad Thursday, because there weren't enough personnel to handle an emergency. The procedure happened when there was a full staff on the floor, ready to rush to his side. The doctor with the correct solution to the problem with Butch's lungs won, and a drain was inserted to handle the infection compromising his good lung. The brain injury, which could have been life-altering, healed with no intervention. Even though most or all of his ribs were broken, he had little pain most of the time. He threw blood clots to his lungs and survived. We were waiting for more information on this. The common thread throughout this ordeal was God's presence—His intervention and His willingness to rush to embrace a terrified wife who cried out to Him for help.

Also, let's not forget the origin of this accident. Butch fell roughly fifteen feet from a ladder, landing on his head and his shoulder. The chain saw fell the same distance and landed on his chest. The tree branch he was cutting fell on top of that. Surviving that with no permanent spinal or brain injury was miraculous. I couldn't stop thinking about all of this. But now we were in another crisis. This time I gave it to God. I had spent many hours in the bathroom in the ICU waiting room, silently screaming and calling out to God. Even though God had spared Butch up to this point, I knew that at any time He could choose to take him. Sometimes that's how God brings healing—by taking us home to be with Him. I've learned this the hard way. I've also learned to trust that His ways are higher than my ways. He is sovereign, and He is good—always.

Sunday, July 27

Update: 5:57 a.m. An extremely quiet night. Butch's vital signs have stabilized. The doctor who headed up the interventions at 4 a.m. yesterday was here this morning. He said he was amazed at how much better Butch looks, even from last night when he left. He said he looks forward to seeing Butch walk out of here. Thank you, Jesus! I think I know a throng of people who feel the same way!

I'll keep it short this morning. It's a beautiful day. Please consider going to church and worshiping with brothers and sisters in Christ. And if you don't have a church home, please consider Abundant Life Community Church Wood River or Abundant Life Community Church Alton. We attend the Wood River campus. We won't be there this morning of course, but we'll be back very soon!

Update: 8:09 a.m. Flat Butch is in Malaysia!

We were blown away. Not only had the Flat Butch movement made it to Malaysia but also to Australia, South America, Canada, Europe, and more. People all over were praying for my husband. People were also praying for my mom. When God's children unite, His heart is moved.

Update: 8:33 a.m. Today's *Jesus Calling* devotion: "Hope is a golden cord connecting you to heaven. This cord helps you hold your head up high, even when multiple trials are buffeting you. I never leave your side, and I never let go of your hand. But without the cord of hope, your head may slump and

your feet may shuffle as you journey uphill with
Me. Hope lifts your perspective from your weary
feet to the glorious view you can see from the high
road. You are reminded that the road we're traveling
together is ultimately a highway to heaven. When
you consider this radiant destination, the roughness
or smoothness of the road ahead becomes much less
significant. I am training you to hold in your heart
a dual focus: My continual Presence and the hope
of heaven. Be joyful in hope, patient in affliction,
faithful in prayer" (Young, p. 218).

Am I imagining it, or does it seem that every day
this devotion is written just for me and my family?

Update: 10:16 a.m. They are baffled. Butch is not
growing any cultures, and they are questioning if
he threw a pulmonary embolism. Gayla says he is
"super sick" and they don't know why. They will
test him tomorrow to see if he can be extubated, but
a tracheotomy is scheduled. Here is what I think:
God has touched his body, and the problem that
caused the crisis yesterday is gone. In Jesus's name!

Please pray that he passes his breathing test
tomorrow and that we will continue on the road
to recovery.

Update: 4:01 p.m. Butch has needed two units
of blood. They don't know why. It could be that
because of the crisis yesterday, they had to push
a bunch of meds and fluids, causing him to be
"diluted." Please pray that there is no reason why
and that his counts will be perfect, just like all of

his vital signs right now. He is "textbook perfect" right now.

Forgot to post this before I fell asleep—update to the update, 6:08 p.m. His blood work shows that the two units of blood did not improve his numbers enough, so they suspect blood loss is coming from somewhere. We do know it's not his head. They will most likely take him for a scan sometime this evening.

Update: 6:18 p.m. Ya know that Mandisa song that says, "He is with you in the ICU when the doctors don't know what to do"?

Update: 8:16 p.m. We have some answers. The doctor and Gayla (our favorite nurse) came out to the waiting room to find me, which can be a very scary thing. Gayla's face looked calm, so I knew that it wasn't devastating news. Here's the deal so far.

They have identified MRSA pneumonia. This is very treatable, and they had already started the appropriate antibiotics to fight this yesterday.

As far as the low blood count/blood loss, they are fairly sure that this is due to all of the fluids given to him yesterday and that he will stabilize. They will draw blood again at 10:00 p.m. to see where he is. Because his vital signs are all awesome, they feel that he is not bleeding anywhere. I'm praying this is the case.

They will do the breathing test early tomorrow morning, around four-thirty or so. I am praying that he will pass and avoid a trach, but if this is what he needs, I'm okay with that. It's temporary and will help him over this hump.

One more thing: Butch is on contact isolation as of today and will be for about a week. We will limit who goes back to see him to family. The best time to come if you want to visit is between 6:00 and 8:00 p.m. Any time is fine, but since I can't come and go as easily from his room right now, I will be back with him most of the time.

Update: 10:37 p.m. One thing about sleeping in a yellow paper isolation gown: it keeps you warm.

Update: 11:49 p.m. Blood test results back. No sign of bleeding! Thank you, Jesus!

It appeared that we had weathered the storm. Eventually we received confirmation that Butch had MRSA in his lungs and in his blood at the same time. This is a lethal combination that kills most people, especially those who are compromised and weak. Butch was definitely compromised and weak, but God intervened through His miraculous touch and through medicine to rescue Butch once again. Next the plan was to decide what to do about the ventilator. He was fully intubated again and had had a tube down his throat for a long time. If he couldn't get off the ventilator altogether, it was safer and more effective for him to have the tracheotomy. This had been discussed many times before, so I wasn't surprised.

Monday, July 28

Update: 5:22 a.m. Butch is doing his breathing trial right now and is perfect. However, they are still going to do the tracheotomy because of the pneumonia. He has a lot of secretions from his lungs right now that he won't be able to clear by himself to protect his airway. I was hopeful that we would avoid the trach, but this will be the safest option for him. We don't want to extubate and reintubate again. The fact that he can breathe on his own now is an excellent sign that he will come off the vent/ trach soon.

He and I had a quiet night. We have answers, we have a treatment plan, and he is stable. Thank you, Jesus.

CHAPTER 10

Monday, July 28

Update: 2:00 p.m. The trach is done. Since this is a surgical ICU, they just did it bedside in his room. He is still sleepy. Later today they are going to insert a filter in his vena cava to protect him from any other clots traveling to his lungs. I'm very happy that they are doing this. I will rest easier.

Update: 6:00 p.m. Butch has been stable all day. He has had a busy day, however. First they did the tracheotomy. Then they took him down and placed the filter to protect against any more clots migrating to his lungs. He also has a brand-new brace to support the fractured vertebra. He looks like a gladiator! Then, because he was still pretty sleepy, I trimmed his mustache. What most people don't know is that this is huge. The man won't let me touch the #mustacheofpower. He is very particular. He will need to get used to me trimming it, however, because he has two broken wrists. Harry helped me with how to shape it, so Butch is good to go.

This is the absolute first time since three weeks ago today that my whole body and spirit feel at peace and relaxed. Each time I've had an uneasy feeling during this storm something has indeed happened. Sometimes it was minor; other times it was life-threatening. Today, peace. I told Butch that he has had his quota of road bumps and that he is required to have only smooth sailing from this point. He has had his share of needing all the attention of doctors, nurses, respiratory therapists, and anesthesiologists in emergency situations. And since he loves me so much, I am confident that he will listen and comply.

They will keep him sleepy tonight and begin waking him up completely tomorrow morning to start on the right foot with the day/night cycle.

Update: 10:13 p.m. This has been an eventful day. Butch has been super busy, and he doesn't even know it. First, a tracheotomy and then a trans-esophogeal echocardiogram. Next, they placed a filter in his vena cava. Then they decided to start the process of waking him up. After that, they attempted a breathing trial through the trach. He didn't do well at all on the breathing trial, which consists of turning off the ventilator and watching what happens. After the day he has had, I'm not the least bit surprised that he struggled. He is back on the ventilator right now and is resting comfortably. His fever has climbed back up, but they will give him meds for that shortly.

Today I listened again to the song "I Will Praise You in This Storm" by Casting Crowns, another song that totally speaks to me.

And I'll praise you in this storm and I will lift my hands,
For you are who you are no matter where I am,
And every tear I've cried you hold in your hand.
You never left my side, and though my heart is torn
I will praise you in this storm.

Thank you, Lord, for inspiring composers to write songs that speak right into our lives.

Tuesday, July 29

Update: 6:25 a.m. It's so difficult to watch Butch cough silently, trying to clear the thick junk from his lungs and his throat. They have to suction him often—very often. I'm praying this junk clears up soon. His fever keeps climbing as well.

Last night around eleven he awoke in extreme pain. I've not seen him this desperate for relief. I don't know if it's because of the incision in his throat, his broken ribs, his T6 fracture, pain from being in bed for three weeks, or what. Probably all of the above. He was very busy yesterday, and maybe being manipulated so much played a role. It was very difficult for me. He opened his eyes and looked at me as if to say "Help." I asked if he was in pain, and he nodded his head, eyebrows furled. If you know Butch very well, you know the eyebrow furl. But this was a furl of extreme pain. So may I call all warriors to battle against pain and pneumonia? He will be taken off all sedation today to try to reset his day/night cycle. I pray that his pain will be better controlled for this.

Update: 10:28 a.m. For the past half-hour Butch has been off the vent. He is maintaining good numbers but is struggling because he is coughing up tons of ick. This is good, but one of us has to be bedside to suction the ick when he coughs it up. This is also good. He is awake and aware. At first he was terrified, but I kept reassuring him that he was safe. That calms him down every time. Now I have worship music playing, which also seems to calm him. Please pray that he will be able to stay off the vent. This will determine the course of his rehab.

Update: 5:00 p.m. Butch is wide awake. He can't talk, but he sure can mouth words. He is asking to get up. So right now I am in the waiting room while the nurse uses a lift to get him into the recliner. Harry is still in there, but I couldn't watch.

Please pray for my momma. She isn't doing great. She's still depressed and wants to give up. I need wisdom.

Update: 11:10 p.m. Something isn't right with Butch's trach. He has struggled all day. At times he is absolutely terrified because it chokes him. Either the tube is too short, it is misplaced, or something. He coughs almost nonstop. Please pray. Surgeons are looking at the situation now.

Wednesday, July 30

Update: 6:08 a.m. It's been three weeks and two days now. I feel weary today—not necessarily physically tired, just weary. Butch had a quiet night after we got through the rough patch around midnight. Today they will try to determine what, if anything, is going on with his trach. They will also try again to wean him off of the ventilator, but because of the issues with the trach, I don't know if that will be possible. It's like it is choking him. All of his vital signs go out of whack, and he panics because he feels like he is suffocating. Last night they had to give him a mild sedative to calm him down.

I am so thankful that Butch is going to recover fully, even though it is taking longer than I originally thought. I honestly thought we would be home by now, but we are still in the ICU. He will be fine. He kept asking me last night if I would take him home. Oh how I wish.

As I sit in the ICU waiting room this morning, I'm listening to yet another grieving family, distraught over the loss of a loved one. I sit and pray for them for God's peace and comfort. Sweet Jesus.

Today I will try to get home for a little bit to visit with my momma. My cousin and I are going to have a difficult conversation with her—probably more difficult for me than for my mom. I think her body is done fighting. She is in pain, tired and miserable. I love her so much.

Update: 10:21 a.m. The doctors have "rounded" on Butch. The leader pulled up his chest X-ray and looked at the trach tube and its placement in Butch's throat. He said, "I can see how this is too short and would cause extreme irritation. We will take care of this." Thank you, Jesus.

Update: 10:48 a.m. Butch has been breathing on his own with only a little pressure help, because he has to breathe through the trach. He is doing it like a rock star.

Update: 6:35 p.m. I had to come to Alton for a difficult conversation with my mom. I left Butch in the very capable hands of Harry. It's so hard to leave him even for a little bit. He has been stable all day. They will do another breathing trial tonight for twice as long. I have faith that he will pass again. As soon as I return, I will find out how he did when I was gone and post then.

The conversation with my mom went fairly well. We have a possible plan but need to work out details.

In that conversation with my precious mom, I asked her to consider entering hospice care. She responded, "That means I'm going to die." I explained that many people go on hospice and then off again. I sold her on this when I explained that hospice care meant she no longer had to do physical therapy. No one would try to force her to eat. She could stay in bed all day if she wanted and would be given medication to keep her comfortable. The panic attacks were increasing in frequency and intensity. I knew she was getting worse, and so did she. But she was forcing herself to do as much as she could for my sake, and she didn't have it in her to continue. My cousin

131

and I planned to tour a brand-new residential hospice center near my home. We had heard wonderful things about this place. Since Butch was somewhat stable, I felt that I had time to take care of this. Carol and I were going to tour the hospice center on Saturday, August 2, three days later.

> **Update: 11:09 p.m.** This trach is becoming increasingly irritating to Butch. He gags, coughs, and chokes. This is supposed to be a more comfortable option. It's extremely difficult to watch. Tomorrow they will replace the tube with a longer one, hoping this will fix the problem.
>
> Another issue has arisen tonight. Butch's abdomen has distended considerably. They think it's gas but want to make sure. This guy does not need any more issues/complications! I'm asking that everyone pray specifically for these issues.
>
> On another note, I am still humbled and amazed at the Flat Butch phenomenon. It's so wonderful to see how the community is rising up to support him/us. I want to say thank you from the bottom of my heart. There is no question in my mind that the prayer support generated through this has made all the difference. I think we need to have a Flat Butch convention in the near future. We could all come together and worship our heavenly Father, who has done such miraculous things during this whole process!

After I settled into my little cubby that night, I could not shake the feeling that something was not right. I lay down on the couch but couldn't relax. I got up, stood at the head of Butch's bed, laid my cheek against his, and prayed. I sang worship songs and prayed some more. I walked around his bed, praying for God's protection. But that uneasy feeling would not go away. I returned to behind the head of the bed and prayed. I also wept. The last time I had this feeling, Butch threw a clot to his lung and had MRSA pneumonia and bacteremia. I prayed harder. After several minutes, I felt a little better, but I continued to pray. The heaviness lifted a little more, so I went back to my cubby to lie down. As I lay there, I heard what sounded like a strong wind being sucked out of the room. After that, the heaviness in the room lifted completely, and I relaxed enough to sleep.

A violent spiritual battle had been fought for my husband's life. The Flat Butch movement (which eventually grew to more than two thousand members) and my cry to prayer warriors all over the world summoned reinforcements in that battle. This type of battle is real, and the only way to fight and win is through intercession. I am so thankful for those who interceded. Ephesians 6:10–12 says this: "Finally, be strong in the Lord and in his mighty power. Put on the full armor of God, so that you can take your stand against the devil's schemes. For our struggle is not against flesh and blood, but against the rulers, against the authorities, against the powers of this dark world and against the spiritual forces of evil in the heavenly realms." Intercession means going to battle, through prayer, against the powers of this dark world and the forces of evil in the heavenly realms. We have the authority, through Christ, to put on that armor and to fight. My friends, my prayer warriors, fought and won!

CHAPTER 11

Thursday, July 31

Update: 6:21 a.m. A fairly quiet night after they increased Butch's sedation, pain medication, and lidocaine to the throat. This was all due to the trach irritating him. I asked the respiratory therapist if he'd ever seen this happen, and would you believe he said no? So it's hard to watch. Butch gags, coughs, and chokes—all because of the stupid trach. Today they will take him to the OR to place a feeding tube and to fix his trach. I'm praying that this will absolutely be the last bump. The good thing is that even though the trach irritates him terribly, his airway is fine and he is able to breathe. He just chokes constantly.

We are getting close to a whole month here in ICU. The people who work here see this often. To me it's been forever. I miss my husband. I miss our routine. I miss summer. I miss sleeping in my own bed. But through all of that, I have deep peace and joy. Even when things looked grim, that peace and joy never left. It's crazy how one can feel joy, peace, and fear at the same time. God's joy and peace have remained throughout a raging storm.

How in the world do people go through times like this without Jesus?

Update: 6:56 a.m. Wow. *Jesus Calling* does it again. I just read this morning's devotion, and this is what it says. Remember what I said in my last update about feeling peace, joy, and fear at the same time?

Jesus Calling for July 31: "Trust Me in the depths of your being. It is there that I live in constant communion with you. When you feel flustered and frazzled on the outside, do not get upset with yourself. You are only human, and the swirl of events going on all around you will sometimes feel overwhelming. Rather that scolding yourself for your humanness, remind yourself that I am both with you and within you. I am with you at all times, encouraging and supportive rather than condemning. I know that deep within you, where I live, My peace is your continual experience. Slow down your pace of living for a time. Quiet your mind in My presence. Then you will be able to hear Me bestowing the resurrection blessing: Peace be with you" (Young, p. 222).

Update: 12:00 p.m. Butch just went through an hour breathing trial. I couldn't tell by his numbers that they turned off the vent. He is on mild sedation, which helps him not choke. He scored a zero, the best score you can get! If he didn't choke on that thing, I think he could do this all day. Thank you, Lord! They will do another trial this evening for two hours. Hopefully he will be able to do it. He gets tired in the afternoon. Even with mild sedation he is awake much of the time. It's so good to see those beautiful blue eyes.

And Flat Butch has reached two thousand members. I can't comprehend this. I am so humbled and excited for him! I told Butch today that number two thousand had joined, and he blinked with what looked a little like embarrassment. This doesn't surprise me at all. It's a very good day!

E ven celebrities had gotten on the Flat Butch bandwagon. The Cardinals' mascot, Fredbird, the cast from *Duck Dynasty*, a dignitary from St. Louis, and a well-known attorney who advertised on TV in our area all had their pictures taken with Flat Butch. I was married to a star!

Update: 2:26 p.m. New casts! The right one is neon orange, and the left one is a dull off-white. However, the left one is below the elbow. This is awesome!

Friday, August 1

Update: 12:11 a.m. Wow. It's August. Butch had his surgery bedside in his room tonight. They replaced the trach tube with a longer one, and now hopefully it won't gag/choke/irritate him. They also placed the G-tube into his stomach. All of this is very temporary. I'm believing for it to be very, very, very temporary.

I would again like to thank all of you for continually praying for Butch and the rest of us. Our whole family—extended included—has been so affected by this event. We have been scared, terrified, sad, and uncertain but always peaceful and full of joy. And even though this has been a terrible ordeal, it has provided an opportunity for us to proclaim the power and the love of Christ. He is so real.

Please continue to pray for my mom. There are difficult discussions and decisions still to be had and made.

Update: 6:32 a.m. It's official: I'm married to the sweetest man alive. Butch had a comfortable, quiet, awake night, and he was ready to talk. I fell asleep, so he had the nurse (a new one to us who is about ten years old) lip reading what he was saying from about 3:30 a.m. until now. She told me he was trying to tell her something for quite a while, but she couldn't get it. Finally she figured it out. He was saying, "Thank you for taking care of me." When I awoke, she said to me, "He is so sweet!" I've been telling everyone that I can't wait until they all get to meet him.

Since he is in contact isolation, we have to wear gowns and gloves when in the room, especially if we are going to touch him. I hate that. It must feel awful to him to be constantly touched with the barrier created by rubber gloves. He kept asking for a kiss yesterday, and I finally lightly kissed him. Now we have mastered the art of the air kiss. I am ecstatic to be able to share these air kisses with him. I am ecstatic to have him.

I have a feeling that today is going to be a big day. He will do more breathing trials, pass them, and hopefully be off the vent once and for all soon.

When I can go back in at 8:00 a.m., I'm going to ask him if I can take a picture of him for all of you. He looks fantastic.

Update: 6:51 a.m. *Jesus Calling* for August 1: "Nothing can separate you from My love. Let this divine assurance trickle through your mind and into your heart and soul. Whenever you start to feel fearful or anxious, repeat this unconditional promise: 'Nothing can separate me from Your love, Jesus.' Most of mankind's misery stems from feeling unloved. In the midst of adverse circumstances, people tend to feel that love has been withdrawn and they have been forsaken. This feeling of abandonment is often worse than the adversity itself. Be assured that I never abandon any of My children, not even temporarily. I will never leave you or forsake you! My Presence watches over you continually. I have engraved you on the palms of My hands" (Young, p. 224).

"For I am convinced that neither death nor life, neither angels nor demons, neither the present nor the future, nor any powers, neither height nor depth, nor anything else in all creation, will be able to separate us from the love of God that is in Christ Jesus our Lord" (Romans 8:38–39).

Amen.

Update: 1:12 p.m. Butch just finished a two-hour breathing trial. He passed like a rock star! He has been awake and talking to me all day long. He keeps asking, "What's next?" and telling me, "I'm anxious to get out of here." I do believe we have turned the corner and are ready to move to the next step. If he can completely get off the ventilator again before Monday, his rehab will take a lot less time. If he can't, he may go to the best possible rehab for this—the Pulmonary Intensive Care Rehabilitation Unit (PICRU) here at Barnes. They don't wait to rehab if he is still on the vent. They will wean him off the vent while they are doing acute rehab. It's difficult to get a bed in this unit, because you have to meet certain rigid criteria, which he does. But there has to be an opening.

I'm still believing for him to be off the vent by then and to skip a step. Amen!

Update: 9:48 p.m. Butch has been so much fun today. He and I have had such a glorious day talking, gazing into each other's eyes (I know, but I haven't really communicated with him for a month), talking about this and that. And he continuously asks, "What's next? When can I get out of here?" He can tell that he's turned the corner. He feels it in his body. Thank you, Jesus!

He sat in the chair today for quite a while. Right now he is on a breathing trial and passing like a rock star again. The new trach makes all the difference. He's not choking, coughing, or gagging.

I can't wait to see what happens tomorrow.

"I can't wait to see what happens tomorrow." I actually wrote that. I had no idea what tomorrow would bring.

> **Update: 9:54 p.m.** I had to make a quasi-emergency trip to Alton to see Mom today. She has had a couple of panic attacks generated from having trouble breathing. She is definitely going downhill. The therapy sessions are not successful. If anything, they are making things worse. She isn't getting stronger. She is getting weaker.
>
> She is in end-stage COPD. We have discussed hospice care with her. At first she was a little upset, but when I explained it to her better, she seemed to relax more. We are considering the hospice care facility in Edwardsville. Has anybody had a loved one there? Please weigh in and let me know what you think. I want what's best for my mom.
>
> Thank you.
>
> **Update: 11:05 p.m.** I am amazed at the miracle that God has done. Butch is beginning hour four of his breathing trial. He is totally back in his mental orientation—no more ICU psychosis—and it's hard not to grab him and hug him so tightly.
>
> We are both exhausted from a glorious day. Good night, and I'll see you around 6:00 a.m.

Saturday, August 2

Update: 6:26 a.m. I slept several hours last night, but I'm not sure Butch did. I have a feeling, based on how he was this morning, that he was awake much of the night. He passed his four-hour breathing trial again with a score of one. I don't know how high the scale is, but zero is the best. He has been scoring zero on all of his trials, but last night his respiration rate was just a tad high. I think it was because he was watching the Cardinal game.

Today will be filled with Butch talking and me interpreting. He has to mouth his words, and I have to try to figure out what he's saying. We've gotten pretty good at this, but sometimes it's a challenge.

Tomorrow my cousin and I will tour a new hospice care center. This may be the solution for my mom. Please pray for an answer that is clear to me when I'm making this decision. I love my mom and would love to have her come to live with me during this time, but it's just not possible.

There are times in our lives when we say, "What in the world is going on? This just isn't fair," and I admit I've felt a little (okay, a lot) of that during this storm. We all have times in our lives when we can feel this way. But with Jesus, a calm and a peace permeate every thought, feeling, and fear. He truly does carry us when we need to be carried. I love Him!

He does carry us. And yet another storm was brewing very quickly, and I was going to need Him to carry me yet again.

141

CHAPTER 12

Saturday, August 2

Update: 10:11 a.m. I received a call from Mom's nursing home this morning at seven-forty. She said she couldn't breathe, and they sent her to the emergency room. I am here with her now. Her heart is misbehaving, and she is basically a mess. I have told them comfort measures only. Not sure what today holds. Thank you, Tyler Pitchford, for offering to sit with Butch!

When I arrived at the emergency room—the one where Butch had initially been taken—I found my poor mom in an examination room with a BiPAP mask forcing oxygen into her lungs. Hospital personnel had taken a blood sample and were running tests. I called my cousin and asked her to come. I suspected that Mom might be nearing the end, and I needed Carol to help make decisions. When a doctor arrived with the results of the blood test, the news was grim. Mom's blood gases were so bad that nothing could be done for her.

I stepped out of the room to speak to the doctor. I told him that we had discussed hospice with Mom and that we wanted comfort measures only. He agreed that this was the best course. The brand-new hospice facility that Carol and I were going to tour later that day was now out of the question. We made arrangements to admit

Mom to this hospital but under hospice care. The doctor told me that when the oxygen was removed, it wouldn't be long before she was with Jesus. Wow. The time had come. By God's grace, Mom had been able to hang on until Butch was stable enough for me to stay with her. We moved upstairs into a beautiful private room and began making my precious, wonderful mom comfortable.

When we got to her room, a respiratory technician came up to retrieve the BiPAP machine that had tortured my mom by forcing oxygen down her throat. This thing was loud and caused her cheeks to spread like a chipmunk's while it was delivering the oxygen. She didn't want it, so we removed it. The technician seemed to recognize me. After a moment, she asked, "Are you the wife of the man who was brought in last month after he fell from a tree?" I told her I was. She asked hesitantly, "Well, um ... how is he doing?" When I said he had survived and was going to recover, she was visibly excited. "Wow!" she exclaimed. "I can't wait to go downstairs and tell everyone in the ER. We've all wondered what happened with him. It was bad, very, very bad. We didn't think he was going to make it." I told her that God had intervened and that Butch was a miracle. She agreed and went downstairs.

Carol and I tried to help Mom get comfortable, but how comfortable can a person be when she is suffocating to death? I asked her if she was holding on for me. She said yes. I looked into her eyes and said, "Mom, I love you so much. I know that you are in pain and miserable. It's okay for you to go be with Jesus, I'll be all right." When I said this, her body relaxed. She begged for pain and anxiety medication, which was readily available. The nurse administered the medication, and Mom drifted into a deep sleep.

> **Update: 4:43 p.m**. Mom's in a room on hospice care. She is finally comfortable. They have given her meds for pain and anxiety. She is sleeping.

Update: 6:14 p.m. Updating from Mom's hospice room on Butch. He has had a quiet day—got in a chair, back in bed, napped a lot because he didn't sleep last night. Oh, and he passed an eight-hour breathing trial with a perfect score!

Thank you, Tyler Pitchford, for sitting with him all day and Kristi for sitting with him all night.

Mom's room filled quickly with family and friends. Mike and Melodie (my ex-husband and his wife) brought food. Tiffany and Jeremy came as did Kelly and Dennis. My older brother's ex-wife, Pam, and his four kids arrived from Wisconsin. My cousins came. We sang, shared stories, laughed, and cried. This went on throughout Saturday night and all day Sunday. My daughter brought my grandson to say good-bye to his nana. My brother called from Florida. I held the phone to my mom's ear, and he told her that he loved her and that it was okay for her to go be with Jesus. By Sunday evening, even though Mom had been kept heavily medicated, the commotion caused by a large group of people was clearly agitating her. She needed a peaceful atmosphere. I asked people to say their good-byes. My sister-in-law stayed with me, and everyone else went home.

Update: 9:12 p.m. God is in this room with us. Mom's breathing has slowed significantly.

Update: 10:59 p.m. Kristi says Butch is doing well. He wants to go home. I am still here with my mom, who is also ready to go home. Her breathing is still slow but hasn't changed much in the past few hours. Jesus is in here.

Sunday, August 3

Update: 4:22 a.m. I fell asleep next to Mom's bed. Something woke me up. It was Mom poking me. She woke up. I talked to her, and she asked for a drink—Pepsi. She became very short of breath again, so the nurse gave her an anti-anxiety medication. She is calming down now.

I am sitting by my mom's bed while she sleeps. She is peaceful. I have no idea what the next twenty-four to forty-eight hours will hold. I will have to split my time between AMH (the hospital) and Barnes. There are decisions to be made about rehab for Butch, whether to stay at AMH for hospice for Mom, or if she lingers whether they will require us to move her.

I am at peace with Mom going to heaven. She keeps saying she wants to be with Jesus and Jenny. I need Jesus to sustain me. I'm only human, and this is starting to affect me physically.

Update: 10:01 a.m. It's so precious sitting here listening to my mom's slow breathing and knowing right now at Barnes that Butch has entered his sixteen-hour breathing trial to see if he can be taken off the ventilator. One breathing more slowly as minutes pass, one breathing ever more strongly as minutes pass.

Jesus has my heart in His hands. I wish I could physically share this peace and deep joy with all of you. I know many of you who read my posts doubt or don't believe in an all-powerful, all-sovereign God. But please consider what this month has been like for my family and me. I've been told I am strong. Trust me, I am not. But the Scripture verse that says, "I can do all things through Christ who strengthens me," is so true.

He is real. He loves you. Please don't let what has happened to my family—how God has carried us—go unnoticed. He loves you so much. Please consider Jesus.

Update: 8:40 p.m. Butch is rocking his sixteen-hour breathing trial. Joe and Kelli are with him. Praise God! Tomorrow he will do a twenty-four-hour trial. If he passes, they will give him a trach collar, and he will be off the vent! Rehab is on the horizon!

Mom is hanging in there. She is peaceful. Part of me is envious—she will soon see Jesus and Jenny.

Update: 11:25 p.m. I am so thankful for everyone who has come to sit with me during this incredibly difficult time. The definition of *family* has become very different in my world. Family is the good friend who never leaves the hospital, sleeping in a chair until he knows that his buddy will make it through the next night and coming every day to be there for him and me. Family is the good friend who calls when he hears through the grapevine that your mom is very ill and offers to sacrifice his day to sit with your husband so you can rush to her side. Family is the forever friend who rushes to your side at every chance, knowing what it's like to wait while your precious mom fades away. Family is the church staff member who goes to Crown Candy and brings a whole group and lunch to the waiting room so you can have a special treat—the food and the company. Family is the friends who drive all the way from Arkansas to be here for Butch and me. Family is the many who, concerned for my health, have brought goodies and comfort items to help ease my stay in ICU. Family is the cousins who stop their lives and sacrifice to help when the situation seems impossible. Family is the ex-husband and his wife who treat your mom (and the rest of us) like we still are family. (And we are.) Family is those who pray and pray and pray, and this list goes on.

I didn't mention those in my biological/immediate family who have also rushed to help. I am sitting here in the quiet of my mom's hospice room, basking in the blessing of family. Thank you so much for being there, for sacrificing, for helping, for loving. I have learned and am still learning a great deal from watching all of you— how you have ministered to us during this time.

One more thing: Butch rocked his sixteen-hour breathing trial with a perfect score of zero. Folks, this is huge. Tomorrow it's a twenty-four-hour trial. One step closer to being off the ventilator for good. After four weeks, I am ready, and I know he is! Praise God!

Joe was sitting with Butch, who had a good day. We FaceTimed, even though with the trach Butch couldn't speak very loudly. I blew kisses to him, and he did the same for me. Though we communicated, we learned a few days later that Butch didn't remember any of this. Enough of the sedation medication must have remained in his system to keep him a little out of it. Several of us had many conversations that he did not remember.

Around five on Monday morning, August 4, Mom began moaning with each exhale. Something was changing. Two nurses came in to assess her. They asked us to leave the room for a few minutes while they cleaned her up a little and turned her. After about five minutes they told us we could return. When we entered the room, my precious, wonderful, amazing mom was gone. She waited until we were out of the room. Sometimes people do this, I've heard. I've witnessed the deaths of many of my loved ones, and I believe my mother wanted to spare me from going through this again.

Monday, August 4

> **Update: 6:25 a.m.** My sweet, precious mommy went to be with Jesus at five-twenty-five this morning. She is celebrating with Jenny as I write this. I am so thankful for the peace, the joy, and the knowledge that we will be reunited soon, never again to say good-bye. We will have a memorial service a little later so Butch can attend along with out-of-town family. Please watch for that announcement. Thank you all so much for your prayers. God is good, especially in times like this.

People tell me that I'm strong. I'm not strong. But Christ in me is strong.

I called Tyler to come and take care of Mom. After he arrived and we completed all of the official paperwork, Pam and I headed for the rehabilitation facility that had sent Mom to the emergency room a mere forty-eight hours earlier. When I walked into her room to gather her belongings, I was met by a technician who didn't realize who I was. She was quite rude, saying, "I was told the family of this woman was coming to get her things yesterday." I explained that I was this woman's daughter and that she had passed away only an hour ago. I don't understand people sometimes. The technician was apologetic, but I just wanted to gather my mom's things and bolt out of there. That's exactly what I did.

> **Update: 11:22 a.m.** Me to our friend and former pastor, Mark Palenske: "Mom went to be with Jesus this morning." Mark to me: "Good for her!"

> Yup. That's the stuff right there. She has no more questions, fears, pain, or doubts. Thank you, Jesus, for dying for us so that we can have eternal life with you and with our loved ones who love you. What a gift. And it's free. All we have to do is accept it.

Pam and her four kids were staying at my house. I went home for a little bit—the first time I had been at my house in days. I lay down on the bed to try to take a little nap before heading back across the river to Barnes Hospital to rejoin my husband. When I lay down, my ears started to ring so loudly that I couldn't stand it. My heart raced and I felt as if my head was going to explode. I can't imagine why. My mom had just died. My husband had been in the ICU for a month, and I was exhausted and emotional. I finally gave up trying to get some rest. I took a shower, put on clean clothes, and told Pam I was heading back to the hospital. I don't remember much of the drive.

Earlier that morning, Butch had asked Joe where I was. He didn't remember our conversation on FaceTime the night before. Joe told him that my mom had passed away that morning and that I had been with her. Butch was very sad. An intriguing point is that this was the first day that Butch could remember being awake. He says he woke up the day my mom passed away. He remembers nothing before this. He believes that maybe my mom passed over him on her way to heaven, signaling that I would be 100 percent available for him without having to worry about her anymore. It's an interesting thought. I believe God determined the timing of everything that happened.

Update: 10:57 p.m. Butch has had another awesome day. I got here around one-thirty this afternoon. His breathing trials are now stepped up to breathing only room air. He is rocking that as well.

Tonight they are a tiny bit concerned about a new fever problem. It's not terrible, but they want to find a source. As soon as I know, I will update all of you.

Today has been so very difficult. Thank you so much for all of your loving comments, expressions of sympathy, and support. I've learned so much through this process—what true friendship and family mean. I've reached a level of exhaustion that I'm not sure I've ever experienced. My body is starting to rebel against me. Tonight I will try to get a good night's sleep behind my husband's bed in my little cubby. This is where I am most content right now.

See you all tomorrow morning, sixish. Good night.

Tuesday, August 5

Update: 6:30 a.m. Butch and I both had a quiet night. After little to no sleep since Friday, my body, mind, and emotional state needed it. Butch has an elusive infection brewing. They can't seem to pinpoint the source, but they are chasing it. After everything that has happened in the past month, I'm not super concerned. They will identify it and knock it out.

Butch is so ready to get out of here. Every day he keeps asking, "What's next?" He wants to get up, walk, and eat. I love this about him. I love him. It's so good to see a smile on his face. He has been experiencing some pain, but they are able to control it so far. I pray that when he gets to rehab this will still be the case.

Thank you so much for praying for us continually for so long. I feel like my family has required so much from so many in the form of prayer and support. We still need it. We are starting to get a little battle weary. It's been difficult to sustain this level of emotion, to handle the physical demands of hospital visits and keeping someone with Butch at all times, trying to maintain our lives and responsibilities outside of Barnes ICU and whichever medical institution my mom was in. I've been blessed that as a teacher, I haven't had to worry about my job yet. I'm the only one in the family for whom this has been the case. All of us our pretty beat.

I miss my mom already. This morning when I awoke, I couldn't believe that she is actually gone. I've known this was coming for quite a while. Her lung function was so poor. If you smoke, please, please, please stop. It's difficult. It will be torturous at first due to the physical and emotional addiction. But I just watched my beautiful, precious, amazing mother suffocate to death. I'm sure that like most who use cigarettes, she thought it wouldn't happen to her. If you want to know what it's like, put a pillow over your face, hold it tightly, and try to breathe. Whether in months or years, it will happen to you. It's the nature of what smoke in your lungs does. Okay, I'm off the soapbox now.

Today should be eventful for Butch. The plan is to try to get him back on his feet. We will see. Even though he wants to go full speed ahead, he is extremely weak. One day at a time.

Update: 8:35 p.m. Butch was in the chair and rocked another breathing trial this morning—four hours breathing room air through his trach. The biggest problem was that his cast was ill-fitting and was cutting into his elbow, which resulted in shoulder pain and numbness in his hand. They replaced his cast, and now it seems to be better. So the next new issue is a urinary tract infection. This is not uncommon for someone in the hospital, let alone the ICU, for a month. We believe this is causing the fever and some discomfort. I hate UTIs, period.

Now he is on his second breathing trial for the day and doing amazingly well again. It's a little more difficult due to a bit of a fever, which makes his heart rate a little elevated. All in all, he is rocking it.

I took a little break and walked across the street to the park for a bit this afternoon. I needed to write my mom's obituary. It's such a difficult thing. How to condense a precious, wonderful life into a few paragraphs? I cried and cried—normal, I believe, for this stage.

Normally after a death in the family, everyone gathers for support, love, sharing, and funeral events. We are not doing this yet, and I'm feeling the void. Tiffany is feeling the void. My cousins, siblings, aunts, and uncles—we are all missing this important part that usually happens fairly quickly. My cousin Barb came over tonight, and the two of us walked to Applebee's and ate dinner together. It was precious. I will be glad when we can finally all be together to grieve, hug, laugh, and cry.

When I walked across the street to the park to write my mom's obituary, I also wrote another essay. I find comfort in writing. For some reason, it helps to put my emotions on paper.

My Mom Died Today

Memories rush through my mind, sweet mommy memories. Tea parties, playing dolls, making playhouses out of boxes and apple pies out of the fruit from the backyard tree. Helping me through awkward teenage years and wiping tears brought by a broken heart. Sacrificing to make my life better. Babysitting two precious girls so I could finish school—more than once. Helping to pick up the pieces of shattered dreams.

I was dependent on her for my physical and emotional needs. She was always there and never disappointed. She was never too busy for me.

Talking. Sharing. Asking advice. Crying. Laughing. Loving.

Sooner than possible, the roles were reversed. I was the parent. I gave the advice and made decisions. She depended on me. I feel that I let her down. Life is so busy—things to do. I didn't visit her enough. And when I did, I didn't spend enough time just sitting and holding her hand.

It's too late. She's gone. I hope she knows how much I love her and how horribly I already miss her. The tears keep flowing.

Love your parents. Sacrifice time for them. Give generously of yourselves.

Wednesday, August 6

Update: 12:05 a.m. Butch passed his breathing trial. It was supposed to be four hours but accidentally went five and a half. I'd say that's a pass! He is weaker today because of the UTI. They let him rest more today. He is getting a little anxious and even maybe cranky at times. Have you ever seen anyone yell at someone without making a sound? Poor guy. Sometimes we just can't understand him. I'd be cranky too. Not to mention a whole month of being in bed, stuff stuck in you, stuff coming out of you, not eating a bite the whole time, depending on people for every single thing, and on and on. And sometimes he's still a little confused due to that ICU psychosis. I've decided that I have my own form of ICU psychosis. It manifests in many ways. When we get home—whenever that will be— we may both need someone to watch us!

It's been a hard day for me. Butch needs so much. I am grieving. There isn't room for grieving right now. All of your loving messages and posts mean so much, especially since we can't gather as a family yet. All of you, my Facebook family, have certainly made it easier.

May I be a little transparent? I have an older brother in Wisconsin who is attempting to detox from alcohol. He is in the hospital, and I don't think he knows about our mom yet. He has been a violent alcoholic since I can remember and has pretty much lost hold of reality. This has been such a difficult situation in my family for all of my life. We've prayed and prayed for him, but it seems he won't change. This is touchy. Please pray for him. God can do all things.

As I write this, the brother I mentioned has been sober for several months and is working on a relationship with God. Of all the miracles I've experienced in my lifetime, this is one of the most incredible. We are still praying, but God has accomplished what we thought to be the impossible.

Update: 6:32 a.m. Another fairly quiet night. I am ready for Butch to get out of here. He is ready to get out of here. The past two setbacks are due to hospital-acquired infections. If he could have everything well at one time, he'd be great. He was in quite a bit of pain yesterday but not from his injuries. The cast on his right arm was extremely poorly designed, so it was cutting into his elbow, causing pain from his shoulder to his fingertips. And if any of you has had a urinary tract infection, you know what that pain is like. He was also running fever from the UTI.

Antibiotics are a wonderful thing. He's had so many, though.

I was hoping to avoid a step in Butch's rehab plan, because he is doing so well being weaned off the ventilator. However, they explained yesterday that he probably will still need this intermediate step to help get him stronger safely. If this is necessary, I'm perfectly okay with that. The plan is for him to go to a rehab facility (hopefully on the sixth floor here at Barnes) to get stronger without the ventilator, though he still will have it available if needed. Then to the Rehabilitation Center of St. Louis (right next to Barnes) to complete his rehab. This is one of the best, if not the best, rehab facilities in the country. Once he gets to this place, I expect him to race to the finish. He is revving up now, wanting nothing more than to get on his feet and get going.

I am so excited to see what God is going to do with him and to hear his testimony once he is out of here. There are so many wonderful things on the horizon! I've known since Monday, July 7, when I saw Butch on the ground not breathing that this is Satan's attempt to stop what God has planned. But we all know that what the Enemy intends for evil God turns around for good! Watch out. God is going to use this whole event to do something powerful in our community and beyond. Can you sense it? Get ready, Abundant Life Community Church Wood River! Ephesians 3:20: "God can do anything, you know—far more than you could ever imagine or guess or request in your wildest dreams!"

Update: 12:30 p.m. Butch (Mr. Grumpy Pants today) has been in a chair and breathing room air since 9:00 a.m. He wants to go back to bed, saying he is tired. The nurse won't put him back, because he wants Butch to push himself. I told Butch this is just like our boot camp class and the nurse replaces our trainer and he needs to do just that! I do believe what he is doing today is more difficult than the "assembly line" at boot camp. Those of you who go to ARCH Fitness know exactly what I'm talking about!

Update: 2:08 p.m. For those of you who understand: I just ate six cookies.

Again, I got a huge response. My eating progress was almost as much of a thing as Flat Butch.

Update: 5:17 p.m. Butch passed his eight-hour breathing trial, breathing on his own totally through the trach. It's difficult to watch because he keeps coughing up this unbelievable stuff from his lungs. It's like a continuous flow. They keep telling me that this is good, but how much ick can one person produce? It's buckets full. Sorry. Gross.

They just took him down to X-ray so they can once and for all clear his neck and remove the collar. It was heart-wrenching. Today he is just a little bit confused, and he was scared. I saw it on his face. I asked him if he was okay, and he said, "No. I'm scared." To take him anywhere is like packing for a weeklong vacation at the beach. It's an ordeal. A nurse, a respiratory therapist, and a doctor must travel with him—even if it's just to go for an X-ray. As well as he is doing, it's a reality check to see this today. He still has a little ways to go.

If they can clear his neck and remove the collar, we've been joking that instead of Flat Butch we are going to have Bobble Head Butch. His neck has been supported for a month. We will see.

As soon as I hear something, I'll put out an update.

Update: 10:25 p.m. Butch is doing wonderfully. I got a great big smile when I went back into his room. During the 6:00-to-8:00 p.m. mandatory no-visitor period, he received a bath. He was fresh, refreshed from his three-hour nap, and happy. We are quietly watching the Cardinal game, Butch in his bed and I in the chair beside him. This is what makes life worthwhile—the moments. The little things make life worthwhile. I am reminded of a Scripture verse that took on a whole new meaning for me right after Jenny died.

"Now listen, you who say, 'Today or tomorrow we will go to this or that city, spend a year there, carry on business and make money.' Why, you do not even know what will happen tomorrow. What is your life? You are a mist that appears for a little while and then vanishes. Instead, you ought to say, 'If it is the Lord's will, we will live and do this or that'" (James 4:13–16).

None of us knows what will happen tomorrow. On July 7, Butch and I spent the day together, ordering a new garage door, buying stain for the deck, eating breakfast at Fiona's. We had plans for that evening.

Our plans didn't matter. A terrible accident changed everything.

My point is that we don't know what the day will bring. None of us is immune to heartache or disaster. At some time in our lives, we all will experience something difficult. It's during these times that you have to depend on God. I have no idea how I would have survived this past month without Him—and with very good friends.

Update: 11:32 p.m. Our favorite, Doctor T, just came around on night rounds. I thought she was going to jump on the bed and hug Butch. This is the lady who, on that very bad Thursday morning when my post said, "Butch is in trouble; pray," came in and saved his life. She stayed with him and us all day. She was so glad to see him awake and doing so well. These doctors rotate out each week and go to different areas. She hadn't seen him for a while, so he looked totally different from when she saw him last. Seeing her reaction to how wonderfully he is doing made both of us feel like flying!

Thursday, August 7

Update: 6:30 a.m. Another quiet, uneventful night. The biggest deal is that when Butch coughs, which is a lot, his heart rate drops to as low as forty. It's not anything to worry about, but they are keeping an eye on it. I believe that if many of us were wearing the monitors they have on him, these devices would show that we do the same thing.

Today he will do a sixteen-hour breathing trial, breathing humidified room air. The next step is to leave the ventilator off of him completely, using it only if he gets tired. We both are so ready for this step emotionally, and hopefully he will be just as ready physically.

I can't believe how many times I've wanted to call my mom to tell her how well Butch is doing. Anytime someone would go to see her, the first thing she would ask was how Butch was doing. I truly believe that she held off going to heaven until she knew Butch was going to be okay, meaning I would be okay. A mother's love.

Update: 8:55 a.m. We are collar-free! This is huge. We also have Maggie for our nurse today. She is the one who took over on the day shift on that terrible, terrible Thursday. She is the one who, on that same day, moved Butch's room to right in front of the nurses' station. She had him for four to five days in a row during that time. I asked her this morning if she moved him here because he was in such danger, and she said, "Yes, but I didn't want to tell you that." I told her that I knew. I wasn't naive about how very sick he was at that time. She smiled. We both looked at him and marveled at what a miracle has happened.

The team is rounding and will get to us soon. I love that now, instead of a half-hour or more of trying to figure out how to help him—how to save his life— we are taking much less time and the conversation is about how well he is doing and about when we can get to rehab. Praise God!

I am totally aware of how close we came several times during this past month to losing Butch. Because I've been here night and day, day and night, I've heard the conversations and watched the faces of the medical personnel as they discussed his case and what to do for him. I've stood and watched at least twice as the room filled with people working quickly to save his life. Many times my knees have gone weak with the reality of how grave the situation had become, but I've seen God in every single situation—every time. He is good.

Update: 2:45 p.m. After thirty-two days, Butch has graduated from ICU! We will be moving to my first choice—the PICRU on the sixth floor here at Barnes. This is absolutely the best choice for his recovery, and I can't be happier. It is very difficult to get a spot there due to the stringent requirements and limited beds. Butch is a perfect candidate, and a bed opened up today. Only God!

Today he is on his sixteen-hour breathing trial, has been in a chair all day, and has done some pretty intense physical therapy. And we haven't even moved out yet! They had him stand twice. Now he is exhausted but happy to finally be doing something.

We are so blessed.

CHAPTER 13

Thursday, August 7

Update: 10:00 p.m. One month to the day from the accident, we moved to the PICRU! The room is warmer, homier, and quieter. Leaving the ICU and the amazing friends we have made there was bittersweet. These people saved Butch's life. They cried with me when he was so sick. They rejoiced with me when he improved. They took care of me as much as they took care of him—checked on my eating and resting, covered me with warm blankets when I slept. They cried with me when my mom died. They are the most caring, professional, personable staff, and they are now family. They made us feel loved.

Butch has his work cut out for him. He will work harder than he has had to in years. It is very possible that he will walk out of the PICRU to go straight home. That is the new prayer request.

Tomorrow is Jennifer's twenty-ninth birthday. I know that this year her Grandma Marilyn will sing "Happy Birthday" to her in person for the first time in ten years. I love to think about this.

Our precious nurse Gayla helped us move out of the ICU that evening. I was surprised at the emotion I felt. Our goal was to get Butch well enough to leave the intensive care unit, but this had been our home for a month. We had settled in to a routine. The people had become like family. So many crises had occurred while Butch was there, and I was hesitant to be anywhere else in the event of another crisis. Butch was so weak that he could barely hold his head up, let along sit upright by himself. I felt like we were stepping off of a cliff.

Friday, August 8

Update: 6:15 a.m. This is the first morning in over a month that I haven't had to leave Butch's room at 6:00 a.m. The PICRU doesn't require visitors to leave. Last night was quite an adjustment. Since Butch isn't in ICU, his nurse isn't constantly at his bedside. He can't talk. He can't turn himself yet, and he can't push a call light. So he has absolutely no way to get help unless one of us is in the room with him at all times, available to help him or to get help if needed. Last night I left for five minutes to go to the bathroom, and during that time he needed someone. I felt so bad for him when I got back. His first word to me was "Help."

We were awakened this morning by the X-ray tech coming in to do Butch's chest X-ray. He is producing a ton of secretions, and the doctor wants to see what is going on with that. I'm praying it's nothing.

Today is Jenny's twenty-ninth birthday. We, as a family, are going to try to gather tonight for dinner. I'm sad that Butch won't be at the table with us. I imagine we will eat at one of the restaurants around the corner from the hospital. I miss having meals with him. I miss our everyday lives. Praise God, this will resume soon.

When I returned to the room after being gone for only five minutes, Butch was in a panic. Plagued by an enormous amount of secretions, he began choking. He had a cast on each arm, so he had been given a special call button, but it had fallen beside the bed and he couldn't reach it. An alarm on the ventilator was supposed to sound when the patient was coughing, but the alarm wasn't working. Butch could hear doctors and nurses talking and laughing right outside his door, but he had no way to signal that he was in trouble. He was terrified. When I got to him, he was choking and couldn't get a breath. I called for help, and someone came in immediately. He was in such a state that he began to vomit violently. I felt so bad for him. Once someone was able to suction him he settled down. This was no one's fault, though maybe the alarm on the ventilator should have been checked. After this, I never left him alone unless I knew he had the call button in his hand. Sometimes we would push it to check to see if it worked.

Another problem that we discovered was communication. Butch still had the trach, so he was unable to speak very loudly. He was almost mouthing the words and had to find a way to get my attention. Many people in this state click their tongues to get someone's attention. My husband isn't like most people. His method: blow raspberries. Every time he did this, he would make me laugh. It felt so good to laugh. I'm not sure he found it funny, but after everything we had been through, after coming so close to losing him so many times, he was blowing raspberries at me to communicate, and I thought that was comical.

Settling in to the PICRU was fairly easy. The people were so amazing and so attentive. Just like in the ICU, they took care of family members as well as patients. One thing of particular importance to me was the beautifully renovated family shower. I appreciated the shower facility that was provided before, but it was in tight quarters with many people sharing it. This was a large, spa-like shower room that made me feel like family was supposed to stay there with a loved one. Again, towels were provided. Taking a long, hot shower was the one thing I did for myself, and it was soothing and relaxing.

> **Update: 9:52 a.m.** Wow. The family shower here on the PICRU is like the penthouse compared with the other hospital-provided family shower. So awesome. What a blessing! When you live at the hospital for over a month, it's the little things.

> **Update: 10:42 a.m.** After almost thirty-five years as an educator, it was bound to happen. Today, one of Butch's former students walked in to check on him. He is a respiratory therapist here at Barnes. We're so very proud.

Physical therapists tried to help Butch sit up on the side of the bed. When they let go of him, he crumpled into a heap. His muscles were so weak. Amazingly, though, when they tried a little later, he was able to hold himself up. Muscle memory is an incredible thing. It's almost like his muscles needed a little reminder about how to work, and they took it from there. But therapists pushed people in this unit. It was like a boot camp. Butch went from trying to sit up to standing and walking a few steps all in the same day. I was a nervous wreck.

> **Update: 1:58 p.m.** Jenny's birthday. *Jesus Calling*: "I speak to you from deepest heaven. You hear Me in the depths of your being. Deep calls unto deep. You are blessed to hear Me so directly. Never take

this privilege for granted. The best response is a heart overflowing with gratitude. I am training you to cultivate a thankful mind-set. This is like building your house on a firm rock, where life's storms cannot shake you. As you learn these lessons, you are to teach them to others. I will open up the way before you, one step at a time" (Young, p. 231).

"Deep calls unto deep at the noise of Your waterfalls; all Your waves and billows have gone over me" (Psalm 42:7).

God comes to us at the deepest level during the most difficult times in our lives. Many of you reading this have experienced Him in this way. All of the storms I've experienced have tried to shake me, but I will not be shaken. Nothing can separate me from the love of my God. Though the storms He'd carried me through during the past month had been horribly strong, another storm in my life had been even fiercer.

Two of Butch's friends and Joe sat with him that evening so the rest of us could go around the corner for dinner to celebrate Jenny's birthday. Jenny is mentioned a few times during the Facebook posts. So that she doesn't remain a mystery, let me explain. Jenny is my younger daughter, and she is in heaven. This is a totally different chapter in my life's story and another reason people tell me that I'm strong. It's another part of the light stand that God has put me on so I can try to shine for Him. During this chapter in my life I was so weak that I survived only because God carried me. I will tell that story very soon.

Update: 11:00 p.m. What a day. First I want to thank Deena and Sydney for putting "Happy Birthday" balloons on Jenny's headstone today. They are beautiful. I was really down because I couldn't go there today.

Butch has been so busy today. He woke up this morning, and the first thing he said was, "Okay. What are we going to do?" He wants to get moving. The doctor on this unit came in first thing and was upset at the amount of icky secretions Butch keeps producing. Remember how I said it seemed excessive? I was right. She called in the lung specialist, who said the pocket of fluid that caused the problem on Bad Thursday when we almost lost him has become like an abscess. The current antibiotic regimen is not covering it, so he prescribed a new antibiotic. I tell you, I can already tell a difference! Butch's coughing has slowed to almost nothing. He was coughing nonstop last night, and it really scared him—and me.

After they gave him two units of blood and the new antibiotic, they got him onto this contraption that helps him walk. He can't use a traditional walker because he can't put any weight on his wrists. This thing allows him to use his elbows for support. There is a seat on it so he can sit right on the thing if needed. The first try was short—he is just so weak. Up again, he took some small steps. Then longer steps. Then almost regular strides—slowly. He walked several yards. I couldn't believe it.

Now I've spent the last hour and a half trying to help the poor guy get comfortable. He's too hot. He's too cold. He needs his nose scratched. He needs his eyes scratched. He wants to roll on his side. He wants to roll on his back. I feel so bad for him. He is frustrated. I'm so blessed to have him that I would stand next to him all night long trying to help him get comfortable.

Tonight our family—minus Butch and Joe (who stayed back with his dad)—walked to Applebee's to eat dinner together in honor of Jenny's twenty-ninth birthday. It was so good to have everyone together—well, almost everyone.

The week's recap: my mom went to heaven, Butch got out of ICU, Butch walked, and we celebrated Jenny's twenty-ninth birthday. Thank you, Jesus, for walking with us through this difficult week. I stand in awe of how good you are.

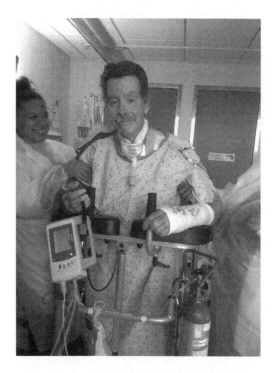

Butch on his feet, walking for the first time since the accident.

Saturday, August 9

Update: 8:00 a.m. Sorry I'm late. Butch and I slept until around 7:00 a.m., but since then we've been dealing with a coughing fit that again didn't trigger the alarm on his ventilator and again resulted in him throwing up. He coughed for forty-five minutes. He's not a very happy camper right now and was very scared when this happened. The nurse said there is an alarm that is supposed to go off in here and at the nurses' desk, but that didn't happen. Please pray for God to calm his spirit; yesterday and today he has been very scared. The culture here is different from the ICU. He is used to nurses in the room all the time. And when they weren't there, they were always watching monitors and responded immediately. This place is a step up from a regular hospital room but an adjustment nonetheless. He doesn't want me to leave the room—ever. He is scared when I leave for five minutes to go to the bathroom. And if I need to go downstairs to get food, he isn't happy. It's crucial that a person trust his caregivers to do well. At this point, Butch is more afraid than trusting.

Update: 10:18 a.m. My friends Chad, Deena, and Sydney came to visit the other night. They brought this amazing basket of goodies, and in it was a devotion book. Today I turned to the section called "Hope." The Scripture verse is Psalm 31:24: "Be strong and take heart, all you who hope in the Lord." The commentary is this:

169

"Hope is not some weak, airy-fairy kind of thing. It takes strength to put your trust in God when life batters your heart and soul. Weaklings rarely hold on to positive expectation for long, because it takes too much from them. But the spiritually strong put their trust in God and let Him lift up their hearts in hope. Then battering may come, but it cannot destroy them. Hope makes Christians stronger still."

The term "spiritually strong" is deceptive. The way one becomes spiritually strong is by being weak and desperately clinging to God. Putting trust in God often comes through desperation. This month has been like that. None of us is immune to life's battering. God is always here for us. Let me encourage all of you who are reading this. He loves you. Sometimes our prayers are answered in a different way than we would like. This doesn't mean He isn't there or doesn't care. God sees the whole picture and knows what is best. His ways are higher than my ways.

Update: 11:00 p.m. Butch has had another eventful day—in a good way. He walked quite a distance, sat in the chair the rest of the day, and has been breathing on his own all day as well.

Butch has the same nurse as last night, and he came in and was genuinely upset and sorry about what happened this morning. When they put him back on the ventilator for the night, they are going to check the alarm. It should have been obnoxious enough to awaken me and alert those at the nurses' station. He assured us this won't happen again. I have confidence that this is the case. Butch feels much better and safer. I'm not sure I will sleep very soundly, however. I don't want to miss it if he is in trouble again.

The funny note of the day: Butch has chosen to get my attention by blowing raspberries. It is quite funny. However, I have made it clear that as soon as he has his voice back, this will be an unacceptable method of getting my attention. Knowing him, that's all the information he needs.

Sunday, August 10

Update: 6:55 a.m. Butch had a hard time sleeping last night. He has such a difficult time being hot, cold, hot, cold. When he gets overheated, he vomits. This isn't pleasant at any time, but on a ventilator it's even ickier, mainly because cleanup is a little more challenging.

The nurses have been wonderful. All day yesterday and last night, they did everything possible to try to make him comfortable. This is difficult for him. He can't do anything for himself at this point, not even scratch his nose. If he is left alone for even a few moments, he's helpless. If he presses his call light, they ask over the intercom if they can help him. (On a floor where most patients are on ventilators and can't speak?) If I'm not in here, no one can answer. Thankfully that hasn't been the case, but soon it may be. I guess I will notify them when I leave the room.

He is a little down emotionally. It's starting to sink in how badly injured he is, what a road he's already traveled, and the work he needs to do to get out of here. It's a little overwhelming. Yesterday he teared up a few times with the emotion of what the family has been through. It's just so much.

I knew what it was like to wait and to worry over a loved one who was unconscious for a month in the ICU, fighting for his life. I didn't know what it was like to wake up one day to find you'd been unconscious for a month. Butch was starting to understand the enormity of what had happened to him, not only the extent of his injuries but the time he had lost. He felt sad about what the family had endured. Such a realization can bring depression and discouragement. He was starting to see that his recovery would take far longer than he first thought.

Update: 8:15 p.m. Butch sat in the chair about the entire day. He is beat. However, each day he does this will make the next day easier. He is getting stronger and stronger. Tonight they will not put him back on the ventilator! He is to the point where he finds it easier to breathe without it. That is when they know he is definitely ready to be off, at least for a much longer period of time. He is still coughing up buckets of stuff, but hopefully that will taper off. It has to, right?

A big thank you to Kristi and Jeff for coming to stay with Butch while I ran home to do some things. I needed to do a little laundry, hunt some paperwork for Mom's affairs, and grab some reading glasses for Butch.

Tomorrow is Monday, and that means he will be doing major physical therapy. He is going to work harder than he ever has. Please pray for success!

Update: 11:21 p.m. Butch has had a rough night so far. I left the room for under five minutes. When I left, he was resting comfortably. When I got back, the tech was in here helping him with a severe coughing fit, which resulted in serious vomiting. It was a vicious cycle: he would cough, vomit, cough, vomit. Horrible. He got overheated as well. It took three of us—the tech, his nurse, and me—to get him through it. I left for less than five minutes to go to the bathroom down the hall. Thankfully he had his call light and help came immediately. This is the danger right now. He cannot be left alone at all until this serious coughing stops. Everyone did what they were supposed to do. I have no complaints. Help got to him immediately. But how incredibly terrifying for him. This is the third night in a row that this has happened.

They say that getting up and moving will fix this problem. I believe this to be true: tomorrow will be the first real day of rehab. Please pray for a restful night now that he has settled down.

Monday, August 11

Update: 8:45 a.m. Super-late update today, but it's because after the prayer request last night for rest, we rested! Thank you. Butch had a couple of coughing bouts last night but nothing like before. He stayed off the ventilator all night and did much better. They drew blood gases today. As soon as those results come back we will know if he is able to continue off the vent.

Today he will begin his rigorous therapy. We are excited and nervous at the same time.

Update: 1:30 p.m. Already a busy day! He has been in the chair for about two hours at this point. He has done occupational therapy with his hands and arms and rode the "bike" for fifteen minutes! He is proving to be the overachiever that I've always said he would be. He didn't just pedal. He pedaled as fast as he could! Watch out.

One more awesome thing to report: I do believe we are done with the ventilator. They took him off yesterday morning at eight. He's been off since. They drew blood gases this morning, and everything came back wonderful!

Update: 2:47 p.m. I'm sitting here, looking at my husband, who is watching TV about all that is going on locally and worldwide. I'm thinking back to a conversation we had earlier today with one of the physical therapists, who shared about a patient down the hall who fell off his camper while trying to clean a branch off of it. He fell about the same distance as Butch but now is paralyzed from the waist down. I stand amazed at God's protection. Every single doctor, nurse, respiratory therapist, patient care technician—all say how very lucky Butch is based on the nature of the accident. We know that luck has nothing to do with it! We know it's God's hand.

Update: 9:03 p.m. Guess who's been out of bed since ten this morning? Who pedaled a bike for fifteen minutes? Who walked about fifty yards? My miracle man, that's who!

Tuesday, August 12

Update: 7:15 a.m. Butch had few to no coughing fits during the night. I believe they finally have found the correct recipe of antibiotics/antivirals for him. The ick he has been coughing up is finally thinning out. Praise God! This has been an issue.

Today will begin with a procedure to place the HOHN line for IV access. After that, the day will be filled with more PT/OT. Bring it on!

I forgot to mention that he's been off the ventilator for forty-eight hours as well!

Update: 4:25 p.m. Butch has had a busy day. He pedaled seventeen minutes and walked five hundred feet (at quite a brisk pace, I might add). The nurse practitioner came in today and said that during the weekly discussion about patients in this unit, it was mentioned that he may be able to go home directly from here, skipping the rehab hospital. Wow.

Here is what has been playing through my mind, heart, and spirit today. Will you worship the one and only God with me?

Update: 10:00 p.m. What a day! Butch has had such success with his rehab so far. Tonight Dennis and Kelly brought me some dinner (oh so thankful to have something different), and we had a wonderful time. We talked, laughed, and cried—all four of us. We are looking forward to many more of these days.

I find it difficult to remember that I can't call Mom to tell her how well Butch is doing.

Wednesday, August 13

Update: 7:53 a.m. Butch and I were up talking until two this morning. It's the first time he wanted to talk about the accident and what happened while he was sedated. This was such a sweet, intimate time. I sat next to his bed, holding his hand. We cried together, often. I shared with him the scary things, and he shared with me how God came to him in his sedated state. We talked about the future. We talked about how God is good, no matter what happens. This was such an incredible gift—to be able to just sit and talk.

I showed him some of the Flat Butch pictures. There is no way he can comprehend the magnitude of this movement—not for several days or weeks. I brought his iPad to see if he can use it. I can't wait for him to see how supportive you all have been and how many people have been praying for him!

Today the plan is to try to reduce the size of his trach. They turned down the level of oxygen flowing through his trach collar (humidified oxygen that flows in front of his trach). He said he feels even better with this. Hopefully another day of leaps and bounds!

Update: 12:00 p.m. A smaller trach, breathing humidified room air only! Pedaled twelve minutes, coughing much less. Staff up here are amazed at the speedy way he is responding, recovering, rehabbing. I am amazed at how God has touched him.

The pace at which Butch was progressing was surprising every medical professional who worked with him—doctors, nurses, respiratory therapists, physical therapists. People in this unit often stay for months or even a year or more. The goal of this place is to rehabilitate patients while weaning them off of the ventilator. Once off the ventilator, patients often transfer to a more traditional rehabilitation facility to continue getting stronger. The fact that staffers were discussing Butch skipping the rehab facility and going home straight from the PICRU was another miracle. We were starting to smile when things like this happened. On the day when the blood clot hit Butch's lung and MRSA was found in his lungs and his bloodstream, God told me that He had him. And he certainly did. He never broke his promise. He never does.

Update: 11:55 p.m. Today has been quite eventful. Butch has a smaller trach tube, which is one step closer to having it gone. He also now has a voice! He has a voice button that enables him to speak. I haven't heard his voice in five- and-a-half weeks. I missed hearing him. It's amazing how different things are when you can communicate two ways.

His body is getting stronger and stronger. He has quite a way to go, but at this point it seems he will be back to normal way sooner than I hoped for.

Tomorrow, they will do a swallow study to see if he can begin to eat. He has had nothing to eat or drink since July 7. I can't imagine that. Please pray for peace for this. He is scared—they will put a small tube down his esophagus to watch him swallow. This makes him so nervous. After several close calls and struggling to breathe at times, this can be terrifying, even if the tube is going down a different path.

Friday, they will remove both casts and X-ray his wrists. He most likely will have one arm recasted and the other changed to a splint. Within two days he will have both of the scariest issues—no voice and no hands—resolved to a point. Praise God!

Thursday, August 14

Update: 9:25 a.m. Happy birthday, Paisley! Our beautiful granddaughter is five today.

Butch and I slept for many hours last night—the best night's sleep so far. It's amazing how different I feel after sleeping an uninterrupted stretch of time. Butch feels great as well.

Today is the swallow test. He is nervous about that camera. I know he will be fine. Seriously, no matter what they do, it's worth it to get some Bobby's, right?

Update: 1:55 p.m. Swallow test about to commence. Please pray that he passes and that he doesn't get too scared!

Update: 8:50 p.m. We take so much for granted. Our health. Our strength. The ability to use our hands. The ability to speak. The ability to eat. The ability to breathe. All of these things were taken from my husband for a time. Most of them have been restored as of today!

Today the trach was capped. Today he passed the swallow test well enough to be put on a regular diet. I can't describe the level of enjoyment he had tasting a banana, a popsicle, and chicken noodle soup for the first time in almost six weeks, eating baked chicken and rice, carrots, potato soup, and apple pie, and drinking iced tea and water. This was hospital food, but it was gourmet to him. His eyes rolled in the back of his head with each bite. I told him it was one of the happiest days of my life seeing him graduate to this and enjoy it so much. He responded, "The happiest day of my life was when I married you."

See why I need him?

Update: 10:50 p.m. Oh holy God, I stay amazed. All on this floor are blown away at Butch's progress. Crazy fast leaps, unusual, supernatural—God.

Tomorrow, both casts will be removed to evaluate the healing progress. The plan is to leave the cast off the left arm and to splint it, allowing use of his hand. Most likely, Butch will have a new cast on the right arm, but that will eventually also go away.

The prayer request is that he will be taken to surgery tomorrow afternoon to remove the filter placed in his vena cava to protect from a blood clot breaking from his leg and traveling to his lungs or heart. Now that the brain injury is cleared up, he can have anticoagulants, rendering the filter unnecessary. The cruel part of this story? He can't have anything to eat after midnight until the procedure, and the surgery is tomorrow afternoon. This after he enjoyed his first meal at dinner tonight. One day this will be funny.

We were told this evening that he is scheduled to come home next week. We were shocked, surprised, thrilled, blown away! Thank you, Jesus. Thank you, prayer warriors!

Home. Next week. Home.

Friday, August 15

Update: 8:20 a.m. The casts are off! The left wrist should be splinted, and the right one will have a cast that is less restrictive for his hand, hopefully enabling more use of that hand as well. It's incredible how dependent you become without the use of your hands. Next on the agenda this afternoon will be the removal of the filter in his vena cava.

He is getting stronger almost by the hour. It's so exciting to watch!

I mentioned that our kids fought and loved each other like normal siblings. What I didn't mention was the healthy competition between them as evidenced by this incredibly awesome cast on Butch's right arm. Tiffany appears to have won this matchup.

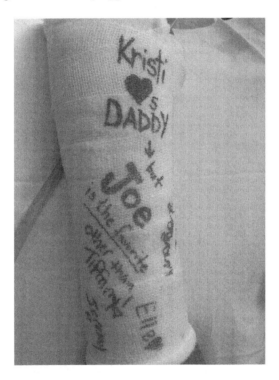

Update: 6:45 p.m. The procedure to remove the filter from his inferior vena cava was successful. He was lightly sedated, so after the procedure he enjoyed a light lunch of chicken noodle soup, frozen yogurt, and two bites of cheesecake. He has pretty much slept since 4:00 a.m. I'm going to let him sleep. It's so good to hear that soft snore—possible only since he is breathing on his own through his mouth and nose! It's the little things, people!

Tomorrow, Saturday, August 16, 2014, is my mom's seventy-eighth birthday. I miss her tons. I was blessed to have such a wonderful mom. Happy birthday in heaven, Mom. Now Jenny can return the favor and sing to you! I love you.

Update: 11:41 p.m. "Evening, morning and noon I cry in distress, and he hears my voice" (Psalm 55:17).

This has been true for the last six weeks of my existence—so many times, almost every day. The past two days I have relived much of this because Butch wants to know about what happened. He remembers almost nothing, which is merciful. He is so amazing. Each doctor, nurse, respiratory therapist, surgeon, or physical therapist who comes to work with him gets a huge thank-you from him. He made both the coordinator for the floor and the speech pathologist cry yesterday—tears of joy.

I love to share the story about the time three weeks ago when God wrapped me in a blanket of warm, peaceful security. He said to me, "I have him." This was during the emergency when they had to reintubate due to possible pulmonary embolism, MRSA sepsis, and pneumonia. God was there. He was real. He was palpable. There is no one on this earth who will ever begin to convince me that His presence was not real. Thank you, Lord, for making yourself so available!

Saturday, August 16

Update: 7:15 a.m. Good morning! Butch and I both slept on and off last night. His medication schedule makes it impossible to sleep without interruption. He is comfortable but ready to rock and roll today.

I want to mention again the pain control issue. We were told by every doctor and nurse that he would be in excruciating pain when he was brought out of sedation and that controlling it would be very difficult. They were going to put in an epidural, but it wasn't safe with the T6 compression fracture.

The prayer warriors prayed, and the pain never came, not in the magnitude predicted. He has asked for pain medication only once or twice since Sunday! This is truly a miracle.

Update: 9:52 a.m. Today is my mom's seventy-eighth birthday. In her honor and memory, I'm asking all smokers who read this to please do what it takes to stop. None of us thinks that terrible things will happen to us. These things happen to other people. But let me tell you no one is immune.

Let me walk you through the last few weeks of my mom's life. Her lungs were so damaged from cigarettes that she simply could not get enough air. Because she couldn't breathe, she began to have panic attacks, which made it even more difficult to breathe. She was terrified. Imagine someone constantly holding a pillow over your mouth and nose, allowing only a little air in. This is what it was like. For the last thirty-six hours of her life, she was gasping for breath but was medicated so she didn't perceive it. But we did. We sat with her, held her hand, and cried.

My mom was the most wonderful, funny, loving person. Of course she had her faults, but she was amazing and I miss her. We all miss her. Without cigarettes, her quality of life would have been so much better the past twenty years, and I have no doubt she would have lived a much longer life.

Update: 11:00 p.m. It's been quite a day. Butch has eaten three full meals plus some snacks. Harry spent some quality time with Butch. Tyler and Gena brought Bobby's. (Yum.) Kevin C., the chaplain for the Illinois Firefighters Association, visited. Joe, Kelli, and the girls came to stay with Butch while I shot home to meet some RHFD firefighters to help move furniture to prepare for Butch's homecoming. The day was topped off with Jeff and Kristi hanging out this evening.

Butch's heart rate keeps elevating. They have determined that it's because he is deconditioned, leaving him extremely weak. This will get better as he gets stronger.

Our nurse tonight is a man who had Butch last weekend. Even with the extreme improvements we've reported throughout this week, we still didn't realize how far he's come since last week. When Butch started to talk to him, the nurse said, "Oh! You can talk!" Then he asked if Butch could walk.

Last week he could barely pivot from chair to bed. He's eating. He's sitting up without support on the bed. Wow.

Prayer warriors, I'm getting beyond tired. I don't have this luxury. Please pray for stamina. I'm trying to eat right and get enough sleep, but I'm starting to feel the physical effects of the past six weeks. I need a touch from God in my body.

Sunday, August 17

Update: 7:48 a.m. Thank you for praying! Butch and I both slept most of the night uninterrupted! Butch's breakfast is coming. (I still can't believe he is finally eating!) The pulmonary doctor just came in and said we would have a boring day today. Awesome!

Update: 12:00 p.m. Butch just walked 360 feet without stopping! This is an enormous improvement from the last time he walked. His heart rate stayed under 120 this time, which is also another huge improvement. Yesterday just standing would cause his heart rate to shoot up over 140. We were concerned, but the doctor said it's just that he is so weak. So Butch is in his own form of boot camp!

Update: 9:25 p.m. *Jesus Calling*, August 17: "Find Me in the midst of the maelstrom. Sometimes events whirl around you so quickly that they become a blur. Whisper My Name in recognition that I am still with you. Without skipping a beat in the activities that occupy you, you find strength

185

and peace through praying My Name. Later, when the happenings have run their course, you can talk with Me more fully. Accept each day just as it comes to you. Do not waste your time and energy wishing for a different set of circumstances. Instead, trust Me enough to yield to My design and purposes. Remember that nothing can separate you from My loving Presence; you are *Mine*" (Young, p. 240).

So many times throughout this journey, all I could do was say "Jesus," sometimes in a whisper but more often pretty loudly! He always answers—always.

Today has been such a wonderful day. Butch walked without stopping for a rest, has been coughing way less, and has eaten very well. He is getting so much stronger. I do believe we will be home soon! When we get home, let's all get together for a huge praise-and-worship time!

Monday, August 18

Update: 9:13 a.m. Late update! Sorry. We've been busy since we woke up! Butch is able to stand from a sitting position without help, but he can't use his arms. He has to use his legs and abdominal muscles! He also walked several yards without the platform walker, which is amazing.

The hospitalists do one week at a time on the floor. The one who was on duty the week Butch came to the PICRU returned today. She walked in this morning clapping for him, saying, "So you are a star!" The nurse practitioner who approved him for this unit said he would be a star, and he's proven to be just that.

Today they will remove his trach. We are so excited. This week will be about getting him stronger and stronger. They may wait a few days to send him home to keep working on strength and independence. This is good. I'd much rather he stay here a few extra days than go to another facility!

Update: 10:36 a.m. Decanulated! In other words, he is now trachless! The doctor now says he may be home Wednesday or Thursday. Wow! Prayer warriors, you rock!

Update: 3:48 p.m. God's timing is amazing. The doctor is working on discharge papers for this Thursday. I am speechless. We don't know what time yet. I will let you all know when he is ready for visitors!

They were talking about discharge. We were beyond excited. This was what we had been working so hard for. Remember, we had been told a few weeks earlier by the ICU doctor that Butch might not go home until the end of October. We felt almost invincible. However, true to the pattern Butch had followed, another storm was brewing. It was almost like we weren't allowed to keep moving forward. There always seemed to be a bump in the road.

CHAPTER 14

Butch was walking around the hallway, which created a circle. The nurses' station was in the center of the floor. Patient rooms were on the perimeter, so patients could walk like they were on a track. When we were at the farthest point from his room, Butch started to feel sick, so much so that he had to sit on the built-in seat on his walker. We quickly pushed him into his room. When we got there, we saw that Harry had arrived for a visit. We asked Harry to wait outside for a moment so we could get Butch settled. I went into the bathroom to get something for Butch and heard the physical therapist say, "Mr. McGill, are you okay?" I ran into the room to find Butch slumped over the walker, unconscious. I couldn't believe it. I ran to him, supported his body, and told the therapist to run and get help.

Our favorite respiratory therapist rushed in and checked for a pulse. He couldn't find one and yelled, "Help, help, help. Call the code. Call the code." He grabbed Butch from under the shoulders, and I grabbed his legs so we could get him onto the bed. It's amazing the strength one has when that adrenaline dump happens. The code team ran into the room. Harry stood at the foot of the bed, and I fell back onto the couch. Time slowed like it did the day Butch fell, a month and a half earlier. I was in shock and disbelief. A nurse was on the bed, straddling my husband, performing CPR. The respiratory therapist had an ambu bag, forcing air into Butch's lungs. The room began to spin, and I felt nauseated. He was supposed to go home in three days. I thought, *How could this be happening? After everything he's been through and conquered, he dies now? Please, God, what is happening?*

I couldn't see Butch from where I was sitting on the couch. The code team surrounded the bed, blocking my view of him. Harry was standing at the foot of the bed, watching. He was obviously as upset as I was. After what seemed like an eternity, I heard something. Harry looked at me and said, "He's going to be okay." I was afraid to believe him. What happened? Butch woke up, looked at the nurse, and asked, "What in the world are you doing to me?" We laugh about this now. But it was not funny then, not even a little. I was petrified. But think about it. This man's ribs were all broken, and the nurse was doing compressions on his chest. It had to hurt! Being a CPR instructor, Butch knows the correct technique. He congratulated her. He said he could feel the blood moving through his heart when she pumped his chest, so she was doing it right. I'm sure she knew that already. The team parted so that I could see Butch and he could see me. I couldn't stand up yet. My legs were jelly. Butch asked me if I was okay, and I said, "Not sure."

Fifteen minutes later, Butch was eating a fried-chicken-and-mashed-potato dinner, and I was having a meltdown on the couch. It was a small meltdown. We'd been through worse. The nurse came in and asked if he hadn't had enough attention that day and had needed to do something to get it. This became the joke of the floor after awhile. But this episode resulted in the doctor sending Butch for a multitude of tests to make sure everything was okay. It was. Apparently Butch has a sensitive vasovagal response to certain stimuli, and this is what happened. He simply passed out. He always had a pulse, but they couldn't feel it, and the monitor he was on must have become detached. I guess I must have needed one more incident to remind me how much I love my husband and how I need him.

The plan was still to send him home on Thursday. I was ready for some smooth sailing, no more crises, no more near-death scares, nothing. Please, Lord, please!

189

Monday, August 18

> **Update: 10:08 p.m.** Check out this Scripture verse: "And in addition to all this, take up the shield of faith, with which you can extinguish all the flaming arrows of the evil one" (Ephesians 6:16).
>
> Shield of faith. Extinguish the flaming arrows of the evil one. BAM

Tuesday, August 19

> **Update: 3:25 p.m.** We just walked around the circuit with the new platform walker Butch will come home with. He walked without oxygen, didn't stop, and did fantastic!
>
> Here is another miracle, and this truly is a miracle. When he comes home, he will be on one medication: Coumadin, an anticoagulant. After all that he has been on, this is crazy. His body has been touched by God—no other explanation. His only follow-up will need to be for his broken wrists. Lungs are good—no need for follow-up. Really? Wow.
>
> Butch is sitting in his recliner here in the PICRU, scrolling through Facebook on his iPad. Please feel free to post on his page! He may not respond as much due to reduced use of his hands right now, but he reads just fine!
>
> **Update: 7:41 p.m.** Guess what? Something unusual just happened. Butch "liked" a post I'm tagged

with. Yes, we are sitting in the same room, both of us on Facebook. Another "normal"!

Wednesday, August 20

Update: 9:00 a.m. Good morning! After forty-five days living at Barnes Hospital, today is our last full day! One more night sleeping on a hospital- room couch. One more night sleeping apart (hopefully— I'm afraid to sleep next to him and hurt him). One more night of interruptions for vital signs and medications. Home. Tomorrow.

This will create a whole new category of updates! I can't wait to share how he's doing at home!

Update: 11:39 a.m. This is neat: I'm emotionally able to start getting excited about the start of school. I honestly didn't think this would happen this year for obvious reasons. Prayer warriors, I have you all to thank and God of course! This is going to be such an amazing year. Things are in better perspective for me with regard to what is important.

Update: 8:53 p.m. Last evening update from Barnes Hospital. Although we are beyond excited to go home tomorrow, the feeling is somewhat bittersweet. We have made friends here. We have gained family here. We will miss these people, who not only saved Butch's life but took amazing care of him—and me. I was texted last night by one of the nurses from ICU to see if I am eating and sleeping. So precious. Another nurse from ICU came up to visit us. She is the one who intervened quickly to save his life. I believe this is somewhat unusual.

So many of you have contacted us about ways to help. Thank you so much! I don't know yet what we will need. So many have already done so much for us. I am humbled, touched, even somewhat overwhelmed at the love, concern, and generosity from so many. You've brought food. You've come to visit. You've brought other things needed—lip gloss, lotion, money, parking passes, cookies, a prayer cloth, gift cards, wet wipes (brilliant), gum, books. You've gotten groceries for my kitchen for our homecoming. You've cleaned our floors so they sparkle. You've mowed our yards, pulled weeds, brought us Bobby's. You've rushed to my side when things got bad. You've cried with me. But most of all you've prayed.

I am very serious when I say that we'd love to have a huge praise-and- worship time together when things settle down and we can arrange it. God deserves all of the glory! There is power when the people of God come together with passion, worshiping Him. Hallelujah!

Wednesday evening we enjoyed visits from two of our favorite nurses from ICU, Andria and Gayla. We had sent a message to them that we were going home the next day. They both wanted to see us, give hugs, and wish us the best. It was a bittersweet, surreal time. We were so thankful after everything that had happened to finally be going home. We had seen God move in miraculous ways. He had touched Butch's body. He had sustained me. He had spoken audibly. And I didn't know this yet, but God had visited Butch while he was unconscious. He had a very simple, powerful message that, in time, Butch shared with me. I am married to a man who has seen and spoken with our Lord. Wow.

Thursday, August 21

Update: 9:21 a.m. Late—sorry. We've had doctors and nurses in here since the crack of dawn, getting us ready to go home!

Estimated arrival time: 3:30 p.m. I cannot believe this day is finally here. Praise God!

You have all walked this journey with us. Thank you so much for everything. It's not over, not by a long shot. We have a lot of work ahead of us, but I'm not worried. God has this!

Update: 1:09 p.m. Our last hospital lunch. We are counting the minutes.

We were finally going home—for real. No more roadblocks were thrown in front of us. We said our teary good-byes, loaded Butch in the wheelchair, and headed down to get into the car. I was extremely happy and nervous. After almost two months of monitors and medical help only a whisper away, we would be on our own. We had borrowed Joe and Kelli's crossover SUV because it was impossible for Butch to climb into our Suburban. We sat for a moment and looked straight up from the patient loading zone where the car was parked. From there we could see the window to the ICU room where we had lived for a whole month. Across the catwalk from the parking garage to the hospital and up a few floors was the window to the room in the PICRU where we had spent the past two weeks. Today, we were pulling away from that hospital together. I couldn't help but think back to that fateful day, July 7, when Tiffany and I drove to the emergency room here, not knowing if Butch was alive. So much had happened. My mom had died. And we were going home.

Butch didn't know that the chief of his fire department had been organizing a homecoming for him unlike any that our community had ever seen. He had been planning this for quite some time, and five area fire departments were involved. As we drove down the road toward our street, we saw that businesses had put up signs saying, "Welcome Home Butch McGill." At the firehouse where Butch serves, the marquis said, "Welcome Home Firefighter McGill." But this wasn't the main show. Our street was lined with twelve fire trucks, lights flashing, and firemen in uniform standing at attention. Reporters and photographers from two area newspapers were covering the event. Friends and family stood in the cul-de-sac in front of our house. Words couldn't describe the emotion we felt when we saw all of this. This was a homecoming fit for a celebrity, and I guess at this point my husband was just that. But God is the true celebrity of this story.

The fire chief and two firemen—the same pair who responded to the emergency call, cared for Butch in our front yard, and lifted him into the ambulance on July 7—gently helped him out of the car and walked him into the house. They did this by design. They made sure he was safely in a chair and comfortable. Once this was accomplished, a line formed outside of our house. People filed in to see Butch with their own eyes, hugged him, cried with him, and welcomed him home. This was an emotional reunion for everyone, but it was wonderful.

Our first night at home was scary and glorious. There were no more monitors to alert us when Butch's heart rate was too fast or when his blood pressure was too high or too low. We were on our own, but we were home.

We had to travel to Barnes two to four times a week for several months for therapy, doctor's appointments, and follow-up sessions. Because I returned to school on August 25, the schedule was grueling. Again, without the help of friends, I couldn't have done this. Harry came over every day because Butch couldn't be alone. Weeks of meals were organized through our church, so I didn't have to cook for a long time. People visited us. A friend who owns a pool company took care of our pool throughout this ordeal. Our yards were mowed. People brought groceries from time to time. This is what the family of God does for one another. All this was necessary for our survival, and it was amazing.

Here's what's incredibly cool: the lung specialist, the shoulder specialist, the pain specialist, the hand specialist, the neurologist, and the cardiologist—every single one of them—said to Butch, "Do you understand, Mr. McGill, that you shouldn't be here? You don't know how lucky you are." Oh, we certainly understood, but luck had nothing to do with it. All the credit goes to God. He guided the hands of our amazing doctors and nurses. He intervened supernaturally when the doctors didn't know what to do. He carried me when I watched my husband cheat death time and again. My husband is my miracle man. One of my favorite worship songs is "Not for a Moment (After All). Here are the words.

> You were reaching through the storm,
> Walking on the water,
> Even when I could not see.
> In the middle of it all
> When I thought you were a thousand miles away,
> Not for a moment did you forsake me.

> You were singing in the dark,
> Whispering your promise,
> Even when I could not hear.
> I was held in your arms,
> Carried for a thousand miles to show
> Not for a moment did you forsake me.

> After all, you are constant.
> After all, you are only good.
> After all, you are sovereign.
> Not for a moment did you forsake me.

> And every step, every breath you are there,
> Every tear, every cry, every prayer.
> In my hurt, at my worst, when my world falls down,
> Not for a moment will you forsake me.

Even before this chapter in my life, this was one of my favorite songs. I led the congregation in singing it many times during Sunday morning worship services at my church. When I fell in love with this song, however, I had no idea that I was singing exactly what would happen. I was held in God's arms. He reached through the storm several times. He was there through every tear, every cry, and every prayer. That's the God I love and serve. He will never forsake us. And I am willing to be put on that light stand to shine for Him, even when it's painful.

This story has an amazingly happy ending. Our pastor didn't have to marry our daughter in the ICU room that horrible Bad Thursday. Instead, on a lovely, sunny Saturday that November, Butch walked his beautiful daughter down the aisle on her wedding day. Our nurse Gayla was there to help us celebrate. Only God could make all that possible. He is always faithful. He is only good. Even when our prayers aren't answered the way we hope, He is good. I've experienced times when He answered the way I'd hoped, and I've experienced times when He didn't. During that chapter, there wasn't a miraculous healing. The shocking, unbearable, and unthinkable happened when my precious daughter Jenny died. God carried me during that time in even more miraculous ways—ways that cannot be explained away as circumstance or coincidence. I look forward to sharing that story of God's amazing grace and goodness, and very soon.

CHAPTER 15

I n my Facebook post at 7:53 a.m. Wednesday, August 13, I
mentioned that Butch had told me that while he was unconscious
he had an encounter with God. He didn't share that experience
with me or anyone else until several weeks later. Because he was
unconscious, he has no idea when in the time line of our story this
took place. I suspect that one of his experiences may have come as
God spoke to me during that early morning crisis when Butch threw
a blood clot to his lung and was sinking fast. I heard the Lord say, "I
have him." Here is Butch's account of what he experienced.

Welcome Home: Butch's Experience in His Own Words

After spending forty-six days in a major hospital, coming home
was both exciting and scary—exciting because I wanted to be near
all my family and friends again, scary because I would not have all
the medical support I was used to having at my disposal. I couldn't
get into our vehicle because it was too high off the ground, so my
son and daughter-in-law agreed to switch vehicles with us for a while
so I could be driven home. It was a beautiful day and I was enjoying
my newfound freedom while riding with my wife, who seemed to
be on cloud nine. I didn't notice all the "Welcome Home" signs
when we reached our small community, but I did notice a few as we
drove down the main road through town. I especially noticed the
sign at the firehouse where my father had been a charter member

and I had been a member for forty years. Then we turned onto our street, and I was overwhelmed! On our dead-end street were twelve fire trucks, representing five local fire departments. I turned to my wife and said, "This just doesn't happen. This happens when you come home in a box!" I did my best to fight back the tears of pride on seeing my brother firefighters.

As we pulled into our driveway, we saw around thirty firefighters in our yard, applauding. Friends and town representatives were also there to welcome me home. Two local papers sent reporters and photographers to cover the story. The two firefighters who were on duty the day of my accident and who treated me at the scene were strategically placed to get me out of the car and to help me walk into the house. I'm sure that wasn't an accident but was planned by my fire chief. I knew both men very well and hugged and thanked them. They took me into the house and sat me in an easy chair. After that, a parade of friends came through to say hi, to shake my hand, or to share a hug. What a welcome home!

It had been a long forty-six days for my wife and my family. Thirty-two of those days were spent in a severe trauma ICU, but my experience during that time was very different from that of my loved ones. For most of those days I was unconscious. I tell people I was in a "happy place," because I felt no pain or fear while unconscious. The first day I remember being "awake" was Monday, August 4, the day Judy's mom passed away. After becoming aware of my surroundings and noticing that my son Joe was in the room, I asked him, "Where am I and what in the world had happened to me?" The next question out of my mouth was, "Where is Judy?" He told me about my mother-in-law's passing, and I asked him if Judy was all right. I later found out that I had spent forty-six days and nights in the hospital and that my wife had slept in my room forty-four of those nights. On the two nights she wasn't with me, she was in another hospital more than thirty minutes away, saying good-bye to her mother.

I spent the next couple of days in the ICU trying to understand my circumstances and hearing stories about my accident and the events that took place in the ICU. People say it's important to be careful what you say in front of an unconscious patient, and it's true. I could hear some of the things that were said in the room while I was sedated. Not only were the words important, but so was the tone of people's voices. I could tell when someone was caring and positive, and I have good memories of those people.

I believe that God allows us to go through trials to communicate a message to us. I'm told that several times I came very close to death. I don't know when these crises happened, but I think it's possible that they came during those times when I had intimate encounters with Jesus.

In the first encounter, or visitation as I sometimes call it, I was in a dark place. There was absolutely no light, but I was not scared. I was in a place of peace, a place of comfort. There was no stress, no pain, and no worry of any kind. I like to describe this state as the absence of all negative emotion and the presence of all positive emotion. While in this place, I thought, *Jesus is going to break through this darkness, and when He comes, I am going to go with Him.* It is funny how you think about what that moment will be like, that moment when you die. I always thought I would be excited to cross over into eternity's light but that for just a second I would realize that I would be leaving my wife, my kids, and my grandchildren. But to my surprise, looking back at this experience, none of my loved ones even crossed my mind. All I could think about was Jesus! This bothered me so much after I regained consciousness that I apologized to my family.

The second encounter was even more powerful and life-changing. Judy suspects this happened when she was watching me spiral downward after a blood clot hit my lungs and MRSA (Methicillin-Resistant Staphylococcus Aureus) was taking over my lungs and blood. She describes how God surrounded her with a warm blanket, and fear melted out of her body through her feet.

During this time she heard God say, "I have him." Her experience was very real, very vivid. So was mine. The timing will never be known, but it doesn't matter. What matters is what God said to me. Here is what happened.

I was in what I would call a meadow. There was grass, maybe a foot high, with lots pretty yellow flowers. This time there was plenty of light! As I sat in the grass, I felt the same absence of negative emotion and the same presence of overwhelmingly positive emotion. I felt the presence of someone walking up from behind me. As the person got closer, I realized who it was and said, "Lord." I couldn't turn around, but I could feel who He was. He continued up to my side and sat down beside me in the meadow of grass and yellow flowers. I couldn't see Him from the waist up, but I could see Him from the waist down. During this time there was a lot of communication, but at first we were not speaking. He told me that He loved me and that He knew I loved Him, and He said that everything would be all right. Then He spoke the word *attitude*. I said, "Lord, did I have a bad attitude?" He said not necessarily, but He described how we in the church sometimes judge people entering the church by what they wear or how they behave. He said this was what He meant by *attitude*.

Then the Lord spoke another word, *love*, and said we don't love each other as we should. He said when we have negative attitudes toward people, we should take the time to get to know them and love them and to understand their circumstances. He said it is our job to love them, and it is His job to change them. I was overwhelmed by His presence and by the love I felt being with Him.

I had been so preoccupied with the Lord that I hadn't noticed His robe. I will try to describe what I saw, but words are not adequate. The robe had many colors, but the colors were not like what you would see in this world. They seemed to shine out from the garment like rays of light. They were so beautiful. Then the Lord removed His right leg from the robe. It was a human leg. I even noticed the hair on it. He touched my left leg with His leg, and the energy that went through me was something I do not know how to describe. It was like the energy of electricity but without the pain or the muscle contractions I would have felt with a jolt of electricity. This pure energy tingled all over. Then, just as suddenly as He appeared, the Lord was gone. I was back in my unconscious happy place. To this day, my leg is still numb where He touched me. I believe it is a reminder of the experience I had in His presence and of the fact that He touched me and healed me!

I can't tell you when this happened; I just know it was sometime while I was unconscious. I can tell you I have no fear of death and no doubt in my mind that there is another place that is so much better than this world. I can also tell you that no matter your circumstances, there is hope. Jesus cares! He cared enough to visit me when doctors didn't know if there was hope. I want everyone to understand that God always answers our prayers, but He answers His way. We must understand that His ways are higher than our ways. I don't know why He healed me and returned me to this world to spend more time with my family and my friends or why my mother-in-law, my dad, and my stepdaughter were allowed to pass on into eternity. I just know that He is a good God, that I have been with Him, and that the love and the peace I felt were something I have never experienced anywhere else in my life. My mission now is to live for Him and to share Him with as many people as possible with the days I have left.

I want you to know that as you read this, I have prayed for you. I pray that the Jesus I have experienced will become real to you. If you seek Him, He will be found!

—Butch

EPILOGUE

I am writing this a year and a half after Butch's accident. He is almost 100 percent back to normal. However, people notice a change in him. He was always loved and respected, but now he has an even deeper, sweeter disposition than before. It's impossible to come face to face with Jesus, experience what eternity will be like, and not be changed! We try not to take anything for granted. Life is a gift. None of us is promised tomorrow, so we try to live like today could be our last. Strangers still approach us and tell us they have followed our story. Almost weekly, while we're out and about, someone says to my husband, "I know you. You're Flat Butch!"

I've often written about the goodness of God, no matter what happens or how our prayers are answered. In this story, God intervened and Butch's life was spared. Earlier in my life, the opposite happened, and my precious, beautiful, talented, intelligent daughter died at the age of eighteen. During that time, God showed Himself to be the loving, intimate, personal Father that He is. I can't wait to share that chapter of my life's story, because so many have suffered the same level of loss and because so many will in the future. Losing a child is nearly unbearable, and without God, I can't imagine surviving such a tragedy.

The relationship that Butch and I have with God through Jesus is available to every person. This is why Jesus came to earth, took on human form, lived, suffered and died, and was resurrected. He loves us so much, and all we have to do is accept Him as our personal

Lord and Savior. That's the requirement. Without this, we cannot have a relationship with Him and enjoy the life full of abundance that I wrote about in the beginning of this book. The Bible tells us that unless we accept Jesus as Savior, we cannot enter into eternity in heaven, forever in His presence. John 14:6 says this: "I am the way, the truth and the life. No one comes to the Father, except through Me" (NIV). This is clear and non-negotiable, straight from our Savior's mouth. It is my prayer, my hope, my passion that all who read this who have not given their lives to Christ will do so immediately. Life can be very difficult, but this isn't all there is! We have the promise, through Christ, of eternity in heaven. We have the promise that He will walk through life's most difficult times with us, and I've experienced this time and time again. I pray that you give your life to Him! He never disappoints!

WORKS CITED

Sarah Young. *Jesus Calling*. Special and rev. ed. Thomas Nelson, 2004.

"I Will Praise You in This Storm," John Mark Hall, Bernie Helms, Word Music, LLC (a div. of Word Music Group, Inc.) My Refuge Music (Admin. by Capitol CMB Publishing), 2005.

"Not for a Moment (After All)," Meredith Andrews, Mia Fieldes, and Jacob Sooter, Word Music, LLC, Integrity's Hosanna! Music, and Unknown EMI Christian Music Publishing, Word Music Group, Inc., and Unaffiliated Admin., 2012

"Oceans (Where Feet May Fail)," Matt Crocker, Joel Houston, and Salomon Ligthelm, Hillsong Music Publishing, EME Christian Publishing, 2012.

Made in the USA
San Bernardino, CA
05 December 2016